PRAISE FOR *HAND*

"Responding to allegations of abuse or misconduct in an organization is one of the hardest—but most consequential—responsibilities of leadership. This little book unpacks this daunting process with candor, compassion, and clarity. It also provides wisdom for how to prepare your organization today to appropriately address allegations that may arise tomorrow. Read it before you need it."

—**Todd Pennington**, *Attorney*

"Praise the Lord! This publication is exceptionally timely—a Kairos moment, in light of disclosure by the media of incidents by large mainline protestant denominations and megachurches having incidents of child maltreatment by employees. As a forensic psychologist and victimologist for 35 years with advanced specialty training in forensic psychology, I found the content highly relevant in providing guidelines in investigation of child maltreatment by religious organizations. This handbook would provide parameters in conducting internal inquiries and child safety investigations, either recent incidents or historical child maltreatment investigation.

—**R. P. Ascano**, *Ph.D., L.P.,*
Fellow, American College of Forensic Psychology

"This handbook is essential for any ministry, workplace, or youth-serving institution. Ms. Sidebotham does an excellent job of explaining how to conduct investigations thoroughly, legally, quickly, with biblical morality, and ultimately for healing. With helpful examples and step-by-step instructions, ministries will be well equipped to handle difficult allegations, develop child safety plans, and demonstrate integrity across their organizations."

—April Gould, *M.A., M.P.H.,*
forensic criminologist

"There is nothing more devastating to a ministry than dealing with allegations of child abuse and sexual harassment. The implications to the ministry's leadership, staff, beneficiaries, donors, victims and the advancement of the gospel can be profound. Theresa takes the big elephant in the room, namely child abuse, and takes her decades of experience in investigating child abuse in ministry settings to provide a practical blue print for a God-honoring response to the crisis of child abuse in the church. Every ministry should not only have one copy of this book but multi copies for HR staff, child safety staff and leaders. This handbook equips the saints to protect and respond to the most vulnerable of us—God's children.

—Craig Clendinen, *Attorney, investigator*

"Theresa and the team at Telios have provided an excellent resource on what it takes to handle allegations. Unfortunately, this book is needed, since all organizations are both composed of imperfect people and serve imperfect people. This handbook will help you protect the vulnerable, do justice for both the accused and the abused, and encourage your ministry to discover the truth and respond appropriately."

—**Jeff Dalrymple,** *CEO of Evangelical Council for Abuse Prevention*

"There is considerable daylight between a ministry's option to deal with an allegation on its own versus trusting its fate with a completely outsourced investigation firm. This handbook does a great job of educating on the process, considerations, and pitfalls of differing responses to allegations so that a ministry may respond to an allegation in an educated and prudent manner."

—**Nicholas Morgan,** *Attorney*

"An abuse investigation can be a minefield of emotions held by vulnerable people. The investigative team at Telios Law navigates these emotions while pursuing the truth and seeking for justice. The process is not easy, but their professionalism, compassion, and integrity have made it worthwhile, and I am grateful for the process they led us through."

—**Anonymous investigative client**

"Telios Law has broken the mold of scorched-earth institutional defense/plaintiff recovery to develop a restorative method of ministry investigations. The Telios method does not conform to the winner-take-all patterns of American law but strives to transform and renew both the parties and the past."

Hugh Jones, *Attorney,*
Charity Counsel

"I have had the privilege of working with Theresa and her team at Telios Law on a multi-year ministry investigation. To a person, each of them has demonstrated a high degree of integrity, professionalism, and compassion in their work of investigation and restoration. I'm delighted there is now a resource that reflects their experience in this very challenging area of ministry."

—Stephen Oakley, *Attorney,*
Oakley Global Consulting

"When asked to review this book, my first thought was it is sad that we live in a time when this book is necessary. After reading the book, I realized that we are fortunate to live in a time when allegations of misconduct by church or ministry leaders are no longer ignored. This is a good development. However, the only thing worse than no investigation is a poor investigation. Everyone who is currently dealing with allegations of misconduct by staff or leadership needs to read this book. More importantly, those who are not in the middle of an allegation need to read this book even more because someday you may be, and as pointed out in the book, many of the initial decisions are the most critical. This book will prepare you to make the right decisions at that time."

—Oscar Price, *Attorney*

Sidebotham's *Handling Allegations in a Ministry: Responses and Investigations* is a thoughtful, practical resource to ministry leaders who must grapple with the unwanted, yet all too-common problems of misconduct by staff and volunteers. A seasoned lawyer, with great depth of experience in professional investigations, Sidebotham aptly provides both a framework for ministry responses and specific guidelines for implementing good responses. One of the book's great strengths is in its deconstruction of much bad thinking about biblical requirements for allegations of misconduct. *Handling Allegations in a Ministry* provides a much-needed guide to this difficult area and is likely to be a valuable resource to strengthen the Christian church for years to come.

—Paul Z. Winters,
Attorney, Wagenmaker & Oberley

HANDLING ALLEGATIONS
IN A MINISTRY

HANDLING ALLEGATIONS

IN A MINISTRY

Responses and Investigations

THERESA LYNN SIDEBOTHAM

ILLUMIFY
MEDIA.COM

HANDLING ALLEGATIONS
IN A MINISTRY

Published by
Illumify Media Global
www.IllumifyMedia.com
"Let's bring your book to life!"

Library of Congress Control Number: 2022915367

Paperback ISBN: 978-1-959099-00-0

Typeset by Art Innovations (http://artinnovations.in/)

Cover and chapter illustrations by Rebecca M. Sidebotham
Cover design by Debbie Lewis

Printed in the United States of America

CONTENTS

INTRODUCTION

An allegation of misconduct—or worse yet, child abuse—is a nightmare for any pastor or ministry leader. The spiritual and moral shock can be so severe that it feels physical. It is difficult to acknowledge that active evil exists in the organization. Sometimes a leader cannot bring him- or herself even to accept the possibility, because of fear or misplaced loyalty. This is extremely dangerous, because it can lead to cover-up and failure to confront evil. This in turn can cause others to be harmed and destroy the organization.

For the leader who gathers the moral courage to face the allegations, there is still the question of how to respond. There are a few ways to respond rightly. There are even more ways to respond wrongly. And how organizations respond makes a huge difference in whether people are harmed (or further harmed), the culture of the organization, and even its Christian testimony.

So many interests exist when there has been an allegation, and they seem to be in tension. The organization must attend to the following:

1. Hearing well those who may have been harmed.
2. Identifying and providing care and support to those who have been harmed.
3. Attending to legal issues, such as mandatory reporting.
4. Creating as safety plan so no one else will be harmed in the meantime.
5. Providing a fair process for the accused.
6. Determining whether an investigation is needed, and all the details of type, extent, and process.
7. Responding ultimately with appropriate disciplinary and other decisions.

Pastors and ministry leaders are typically not trained to deal with these issues. Some people spend decades in ministry and never have serious allegations come up. (Others end up in a role where they deal with them all the time.) Unfortunately, the intuitive response in these situations is usually the wrong one, erring in one direction or another. Common mistakes including failing to hear victims adequately, failing on privacy and confidentiality issues, and failing to treat people accused with fairness.

This handbook is intended to help pastors, ministry leaders, and board members walk through the process. Except in simple situations with very minor allegations, it may not be a do-it-yourself process. We shouldn't be surprised by this, since the Body of Christ isn't designed to depend on individuals. The information presented here will help guide you in determining what kind of help you need and when.

This handbook is also for lawyers, members of law enforcement, and forensic practitioners who find themselves investigating allegations of misconduct at houses of worship. This book is intended to help investigators maintain a just, biblically based, and legally sound approach to addressing and preventing future allegations of misconduct.

An allegation is usually about evil of some kind and involves an attack on the innocence of children or other vulnerable people. At the same time, an allegation of such evil, or the mismanagement in responding to one, affects the good reputation of the organization. Even more important than taking the right practical steps is to address the situation in prayer. A confidential prayer team can support all the organization's actions, praying for wisdom in acting rightly, the truth to come out, healing for those harmed, and God to act redemptively.

Part of the work of Christ can be seen as an investigative response:

I will give you as a covenant for the people,
a light for the nations,
to open the eyes that are blind,

to bring out the prisoners from the dungeon,
from the prison those who sit in darkness.[1]

Throughout the chapters, you will read both fictional and real-world case examples, biblical references, and practical advice for addressing the key components of any ministry allegation. Chapter 1 discusses receiving complaints and how to establish reporting systems to encourage reporting. Chapter 2 focuses on the decision-making that goes into pursuing an investigation or not. Chapter 3 discusses different ways to structure investigations and which structures are appropriate in different situations. Chapter 4 details special considerations of child abuse allegations. Chapter 5 explains the processes of building an investigative team. Chapter 6 outlines how an investigation progresses. Chapter 7 addresses concerns of memory and credibility issues. Chapter 8 focuses on responsibly handling investigative documents. Chapter 9 explains when and how to bring an ongoing investigation to a close. Chapter 10 focuses on leadership responsibilities, restoration, and reconciliation within a congregation.

CHAPTER 1

REPORTS AND COMPLAINTS

A Report of Sexual Harassment

arah works at Everyone's Bible Church (EBC) as an executive assistant to Pastor Flirt, an associate pastor on staff. She is single, and he is married. Sarah is fairly shy and quiet. A few months ago, Pastor Flirt started making comments about how pretty she is. That made her uncomfortable, but she didn't say anything at first. Then he escalated to sending her texts of a sexual nature. She did respond by text and ask him not to. He stopped for a month or two, then started again. Slowly, the texts became more graphic.

Sarah shared her problem with the Director of Children's Ministry, Kate, who offered sympathy and suggested that Sarah approach the senior pastor, Pastor Responsible, but did not otherwise provide any practical support. Finally, Sarah did tell Pastor Responsible she was uncomfortable with some of the comments Pastor Flirt had made, but she was too shy to give details. She asked if she could switch jobs to work for someone else. Pastor Responsible did not ask for details or to see the text messages. He told Sarah that she should confront Pastor Flirt directly per Matthew 18[1] and that he would not get involved until Sarah had carried out this process. Was this the right approach?

Concerns with Child Safety Boundaries

EBC has a great kids' ministry, with many committed volunteers. For instance, Elder Close loves kids, and they love him too. He is a familiar figure working in the children's ministry, and children flock to him. The church is grateful to him for the countless hours he spends with kids.

One day, Elder Law came to Pastor Responsible and said, "While I know we all appreciate how Elder Close works with kids, I am somewhat concerned. Last Sunday, I saw him sitting with little Annie, who is six years old, on his lap. In the coffee time after church, Emmie, who is 10, ran up to him. As he was talking to people, she leaned against him, and he began rubbing her chest."

Pastor Responsible's first thought was, *Elder Close just loves kids. That's how he is. I know they sit on his lap and he is very affectionate. But that's just him. If there was anything wrong with it, I'm sure the kids wouldn't run up to him. Also, he is a man of high character who happens to give a lot of money to the church.*

After thinking about the situation some more, Pastor Responsible realized, *This is somewhat concerning, since it's against our child protection policies to have a child of that age sit on an adult's lap or to touch children that intimately. We should immediately discuss this with our child safety coordinator.*

Pastor Responsible then set up a meeting for later that day with Elder Law, himself, and the child safety coordinator.

Encouraging Reports and Complaints

Nobody likes complaints, including organizational leadership. Despite this instinctive reaction, an organization should encourage internal complaints and whistleblowing anyway. There are multiple reasons.

First, we want to root out misconduct, whether that involves child safety, sexual harassment, or ethical issues involving finances. Immoral or dubious behavior takes hold if no one feels free to report it or discuss it.

Second, organizations that address and resolve conflicts internally are less likely to have to deal with their scandals in the public square. Social media, law enforcement, a government agency, or the media are not pleasant forums for resolving problems.

Third, when organizations routinely encourage and address internal complaints and no negative action is taken toward the complaining employees, they are likely to have a better workplace, where people feel safe and cared for. In addition, they are less likely to get retaliation claims.

Fourth, it is a legal defense to some discrimination claims if an organization has a known complaint procedure that employees have not used. This is particularly true if the organization has a track record of helpful responses for those who previously did use the complaint system.

Fifth, victims of crimes and other inappropriate conduct struggle to disclose the misconduct. Many victims never disclose their abuse— they may want to but do not know how. A common barrier is the fear that they will not be believed, and then ostracized and outcast as being liars. In some instances, allegations are disclosed but in the form of gossip. This leads to damaged reputations, mass fear, and a breakdown of trust within the congregation. Having clear processes for disclosure and trained members, elders, and clergy who know what to do when an allegation is disclosed to them protects both those bringing allegations and the accused.

Finally, if leaders want a safe and ethical organization, people must feel free to discuss dilemmas and shortcomings. Organizations with mechanisms for facing truth tend to be healthier. They get the behaviors they reward.

How to Set Up the Reporting Process

Reporting could cover issues including: sexual harassment, discrimination, child safety, conduct and discipline, unethical business practices, unsafe conditions, suspected violations of securities laws (if that applies), social media misuse, and computer use/electronic information. Conduct and discipline policies must also prohibit retaliation to be legal and effective. A formal whistleblower policy is a helpful idea.

It is advisable to have a standard formal procedure for all complaints and grievances. There should be at least two persons to report to, so a backup individual is available if the first person is the subject of the complaint or the person making the complaint is otherwise reluctant to talk to him or her. Probably your attorney should not be one of the two people receiving complaints. Setting aside the cost of having your attorney field complaints, you don't want to make your attorney into a fact witness—the best use of your attorney is to provide you with advice. If the organization is sizable, a complaint hotline can be a good idea.

The policy can encourage complaints in writing. Encouraging a written grievance or complaint is effective because it encourages people to document their requests and can help in setting up an investigation. Ideally, any written complaint should include as much information as possible: the dates, times, setting, and people involved; a detailed description of the allegation and the context in which it occurred; if this is an isolated incident, a pattern, or an escalation; whether anyone has been notified; and the nature of the relationship between the reporter and the reported. But the organization should also accept complaints verbally and document the complaints in detail

Complaints should be treated respectfully. If supervisors can receive complaints, when should they involve HR or other leadership? Supervisors may deal with minor problems directly but should notify HR or leadership about even minor allegations of discrimination or harassment, particularly if an investigation may be needed. Complaints should be stored securely with limited access for only those who have a need to know.

Values to Be Addressed

Four principles should be considered in responding to a report or setting up an investigation.[2] The first is to protect the person who may be a victim. As we will discuss further, this may involve administrative leave or other safety measures. In this context, the complaint or report should be treated as if it were true.

The second principle is to seek justice for the alleged victim. In a child abuse case, this may be carried out by law enforcement or child protective services (after a mandated report), but in other cases, the organization may need to carry out an investigation. However, justice for the victim can also include a compassionate approach and putting needed support into place, which we will discuss further.

The third principle is to seek justice for the accused. This may involve bringing the accused to justice, but it should also involve giving justice to the accused in the process. An allegation is just that—it may not be true.

In order to pursue justice for both the alleged victim and the alleged offender, the investigation should take a neutral stance. Allegations should be treated as if they may be true, but without a presumption that they are true. Neither is there a presumption of innocence, such as with a criminal trial. Investigations start from a neutral position.

A fourth principle is to protect the organization, which is also a fiduciary duty of the organization. Protecting the organization is complex. The organization should protect its core religious mission and calling, which means acting with integrity and doing the right thing. A religious organization is not carrying out its calling if it allows injustice to continue or the innocent to be harmed.

An organization's calling will likely involve efforts to protect and care for those who may have been harmed. The organization should also protect against reputational and legal harm, dealing with issues in a responsible way according to best practices. The organization should respond by caring for people, but is not obliged to do so in a way that creates great legal or financial risk. Setting up an investigation in a way that creates more risk likely violates fiduciary duties to the nonprofit.

The Opportunity Offered by Misconduct Allegations

Allegations of misconduct, especially leadership misconduct, are one of the hardest things for ministries to handle, bringing shock and grief. A common response is to fail to act on allegations, fail to take them seriously, or push the person harmed into dealing with the offender directly. If the problem is not adequately documented and addressed, it can sometimes go on for years, to the detriment of the organization.

Misconduct allegations can relate to and impact employees, members of the organization, or both. Yet allegations offer a great opportunity to seek truth and justice and minister to people. An allegation handled well shows people the ministry cares and has integrity. It also protects victims from further harm, protects the organization from legal liability, and does justice to the accused. If quick intervention and treatment occur where there has been child abuse, for instance, much of the lasting trauma may be avoided.

Provide clearly defined ways to report allegations of misconduct.[3] Make sure complaints are taken seriously and not ignored. Waiting to respond can allow harm to continue. Even if employees want to keep their allegations confidential, doing so should not be an option under organizational policies, because others may be put at risk.

Responding correctly and offering spiritual care can move the organization forward. This creates a culture where the voices of victims can be heard and ungodly behavior is confronted. In short, misconduct allegations offer a chance to walk in the light. Responding and investigating well also protects from legal liability. But that is secondary to responding and caring well for people.

Crisis Response Team

Depending on the nature of the allegations, a crisis response team may be helpful. This could be overkill for a standard problem that HR might deal with, but could be useful in situations likely to have ramifications or where no dedicated professionals available to assist. Such a team could include: executive leader, project manager, advocacy member to communicate with victims or their families, child safety coordinator (in the case of child abuse), communications spokesperson, or legal counsel. Response team members should not have a close relationship creating a conflict of interest with someone who is accused or an alleged victim.

The response team ensures that reporting requirements have been met, plans how to handle internal and external communications, considers the need for an investigation, and discusses legal issues.

Checking Legal Standards

Once the complaint has been made, leaders will consider a response, which may include an investigation. Leaders will want to examine legal standards involved—state and federal laws and regulations that apply to this situation. They may want to consult counsel about the potential for legal liability and any legal requirements.

Equal Employment Opportunity Commission (EEOC) guidance documents are a good resource in employment situations. Where there are child abuse allegations, reporting standards control and other best practices should be followed.

The team will also have to balance reasonable expectations of privacy and data protection laws (created by common law or statutory requirements from a number of countries) with the needs of the investigation.

Getting Legal Advice

If an investigation is just for fact-finding and you have no need for an evaluation of legal consequences, you may not need an attorney. Also, if the investigation is extremely simple and you cannot imagine any way it could turn into a lawsuit, seeking an attorney's advice may not be warranted.

If, on the other hand, you have some concerns about legal analysis of consequences, liability risk, and remedial options, you should work with an attorney. If an investigation is triggered because a lawsuit or administrative charge has been filed, legal counsel should most certainly be involved. What is more, if the situation is potentially explosive or could threaten the existence of your organization, you may need an attorney deeply involved. Your counsel should be able to help you think through an appropriate response and the possible ramifications of your investigation.

You may want legal advice about several areas, such as how to:

1. Conduct the investigation so that it is well executed and also protected.
2. Comply with statutory requirements.
3. Avoid serious legal consequences.

You may wish to have an attorney qualified in working on investigations supervise or conduct the investigation. Legal advice can protect important policy discussions under the attorney-client privilege.[4] Finally, having an attorney involved may also mean that the work of the investigation is protected as the attorney's work product.[5]

Often, religious organizations would prefer not to have an attorney involved because the cost can run from several thousand to tens of thousands of dollars or more, depending on the scope of the work. Be aware that even one lawsuit will range from tens of thousands (just in the beginning stages) to many hundreds of thousands to litigate, and that is not even counting what a victim may recover. Although insurance may pay some or all of these costs, the cost to the organization is also very high in terms of time and allocation of resources.

Consider the level of risk: risk to reputation, risk of legal challenge, financial risk, and risk of failing to carry out the investigation competently. Do you need an attorney to advise on these issues?

How Should an Attorney Advise a Religious Organization?

All attorneys are subject to ethical rules that inform their duties to clients, courts, and other parties. Much like the professional rules that govern doctors, therapists, and other licensed professionals, the ethical rules that bind attorneys are intended to ensure that attorneys provide competent and effective representation to their clients in a manner that is conducive to a fair and equitable legal system as a whole. When attorneys break these ethical rules, they are subject to suspension or revocation of their law license as well as personal liability for legal malpractice.

One of those ethical rules provides as follows:

> In representing a client, a lawyer shall exercise independent professional judgment and render candid advice. In rendering advice, a lawyer may refer not only to law but to other considerations such as moral, economic, social and political factors, that may be relevant to the client's situation.[6]

Under this rule, attorneys should advise clients from a holistic perspective that takes into account not only legal liability and financial risk, but also morality and compassion. Applying this rule in the context of responding to abuse, attorneys for ministries should not be concerned solely with preventing liability for a ministry client or conserving its financial resources. Rather, attorneys should advise their ministry clients in a way that emphasizes a course of action that is moral, honest, and compassionate.

A morally upright response to abuse may not always be the easiest path to avoiding liability or saving money. But the best interest of a ministry means doing what is consistent with that organization's vision and values, especially when it comes to responding compassionately to victims of abuse.

Administrative Leave and Safety Responses

If someone has been accused, should the person be put on leave? This question brings up a related question: Are there any safety issues involved? This is one of the first things that an employer should figure out when there has been a complaint or questionable behavior is observed. The issues involved will likely define the need for administrative leave.

In some situations, the allegations are so serious that the person may need to be put on leave, even if that means a change of international placement pending further investigation. Some examples of this include egregious sexual misconduct, child abuse, allegations involving violent behavior, or where the accused persons are a danger to themselves or others around them. Usually, this should be paid leave, so that it is not punitive (before anything has been substantiated). The key question here is physical and emotional safety for all involved. Usually paid leave is not an adverse employment action,[7] though unpaid leave could be.[8]

Putting someone on leave is not necessary in all circumstances. In some situations, the person may be able to work from home. Or arrangements can be made so that the person accused and the reporting person do not have to work together. Or limitations can be put in place about the type of work the person can do (e.g., they may not interact with children).

Another consideration is whether this is an allegation limited by time and geography (such as an incident in the office) and can be investigated quickly, or whether it will be far-flung and take months or even years to determine what happened.

With all allegations of misconduct, for a credible investigation or response, a leader who is accused and those very close to that leader should lose the ability to influence decision-making. Independent board members or other unbiased leadership should take over. With recusal, any exoneration will be much more compelling and corrective actions much less messy. Certainly, others may grow suspicious if the alleged offender is still an active member of leadership when the leadership team comes to the conclusion that the alleged offense did not happen.

Policies should be created to be sure similar situations are treated the same and to give the decision-makers some help in making these judgment calls.

What about Matthew 18?

While Matthew 18:15 is a great scriptural guide on how to handle disputes and personal differences between Christians, it has limitations. First, it describes a process between persons of equal status. Both in biblical times and today, other approaches are described for persons of little power, such as Paul's advocating for Onesimus to Philemon. Second, this approach doesn't address criminal activity, breaking the law, or danger to the public. Most churches would not use the Matthew 18 directive in the case of robbery, rape, or murder.

Misapplying Matthew 18 may force people, even children, inappropriately into a context where they have to confront an offender.

Those reporting abuse or misconduct should not have to put themselves in undue danger, physically or emotionally, to bring allegations to leadership. If a victim of wrongdoing is afraid the offender will retaliate, and the policy is too strict on enforcing the Matthew 18 model, then the victim may just not report it and choose instead to simply leave or do nothing. This could result in continued abuse going unnoticed.

If the allegation is of child abuse, then mandatory reporting must be carried out immediately and a Matthew 18 context should not even be considered. Failure to report to law enforcement or child protective services is often a criminal offense, and reporting must be done quickly to comply with the law.

For allegations that may be criminal but are brought by adults, alleged victims can be advised to report or assisted to report, as appropriate. See Appendix B for more discussion of scriptural principles.

Pastoral Care for Those Involved

When there has been a serious allegation, such as of child abuse, pastoral care needs arise quickly. The safety plan may involve the accused being put on administrative leave or not being allowed to attend church or be involved in ministry. A family that has just found out about an allegation of child abuse will be devastated. A victim of child abuse or sexual assault will suffer his or her own trauma. Ministers and leaders are also suffering from shock and trauma. How do we care for people?

First, the care needs of those involved should be thoroughly and sensitively evaluated. The organization will want to provide that care. But no one person or group can care for everyone. For one thing, it would be too much of an emotional burden. It would also lead to bias one way or the other. If one person's story is believed, it is likely that the other "side" will not be believed. In the past, this has led to disregarding victims at the expense of offenders, or completely neglecting care of those accused in favor of those who may have been harmed.

Caring for someone who may have been harmed is the highest priority. This can be the child or individual who may have been abused, but could also include his or her immediate family as collateral victims. From leadership, this should invoke a warm response, compassionately hearing the person's story and checking in regularly to see what the needs are. It is likely that professional help will be needed. This help should come from a source that can unconditionally accept the person's story of abuse. Therefore, it should be differentiated from those responsible for overseeing or being involved in any investigation. Therapeutic or pastoral support in areas such as spiritual resiliency may also be helpful.

People may not understand how to appropriately respond to abuse victims and their families. The organization's plan should be developed in conjunction with an expert on protecting abuse victims. Trained individuals will have skills such as: active listening, knowledge of trauma, knowledge of appropriate referrals in the community, knowledge of practical resources available, and how to avoid secondary victimizations. The organization can also provide practical help to the family of someone who may have been harmed, such as transportation, meals, and meeting other practical needs.

The organization can partner with community organizations that have expertise in offering psychological and spiritual care for victims. If there is a court case, the organization can support those who may have been harmed through that process.

Caring for the accused is also important. Being accused, whether the person is guilty or innocent, is a painful experience. Leadership will want to respond to a person accused with kindness and without assuming guilt. However, directly providing care will lead to a conflict of interest, as leadership is responsible to be impartial in steps forward, like the investigation or assisting law enforcement. Therefore, a care plan should be set up for someone accused. This should be provided by someone who will not be a decision-maker, will not be involved in the investigation, and who is free to unconditionally accept the position of the accused.

If the accused says that he is innocent, this person can accept that and proceed accordingly with pastoral care. If a person accused is going to be removed from the ministry for any length of time, compassionate care is especially important. It may also be appropriate to refer to a clinician with training in sexual boundary violation for diagnosis or care.

Caring for others involved may be less urgent but is also important. When any ministry has to face allegations of abuse or serious misconduct, it is a shock and some level of trauma for all involved. This is particularly true for ministry leaders who have to respond. They may be grieving that someone they know or love is or could be an offender. They may be shocked at the harm done or disbelieving that it happened.

It is not uncommon for survivors to attack ministry leaders (justly or unjustly) because of their own trauma, and they can say some nasty things. Such attacks may be made publicly, which makes them even more painful. Ministry personnel need help on a practical level to navigate and respond to the allegations, which could come from an attorney or a consultant. They also need to have their trauma spiritually and emotionally addressed. This could come through a support team or pastoral or psychological counseling. Sometimes someone does not have the gifting and emotional resilience to walk through these situations, and needs to be placed into a different role for their own protection.

Caring for other members or a congregation is also important. While they may not be as directly involved, it is still difficult. For some, the situation may trigger their own trauma or memories of past abuse. For members who are somewhat removed, it is still important to consider what updates they should have, and also to make available resources for them, such as pastoral counseling.

Retaliation May Be Complicated

Tom and Sally have worked for a missionary organization, Everybody Everywhere, for several years. In that time, they have made numerous complaints about the conduct of their teammates and are seen to be very critical and suspicious. Bill, their leader, does his best to smooth things over between them and other teammates, but he too is getting increasingly frustrated with them.

Tom and Sally go to their employer, the mission leader, with a complaint about Bill. They allege that Bill hasn't been following the regulations, and there are hints that he may have broken some laws. The mission leader investigates it to the best of her ability and finds no substance for Tom and Sally's allegations. The mission leader tells Tom and Sally that, and they accuse her of covering up Bill's illegal activity. The two consider filing a complaint about the mission leader but are not sure who would receive such a complaint.

Shortly after, the mission leader asks them to leave the organization. They do, with much upheaval, alleging that the mission leader is in collusion with Bill. A few weeks later, the mission leader is surprised to receive a complaint from Tom and Sally's attorney indicating that the organization may have violated whistleblower regulations. The attorney is demanding that they send him the latest policy and guidelines so he can read what the policies are regarding whistleblowing.

The Law and Whistleblowing

Retaliation against whistleblowers happens fairly often.[9] Retaliation is one of the hottest reasons for employment litigation, because the underlying complaint doesn't even have to be true.

We won't even try to cover the whistleblower statutes—a patchwork of federal and state statutes that protect people making complaints. Some of the statutes provide financial benefits for the whistleblower— roughly, if the government can recover money against the company, the whistleblower gets a cut. In our hypothetical depiction, with the reporting person saying the leader may have broken laws, that scenario might be developing.

Civil rights and employment statutes, such as Title VII and the National Labor Relations Board, also protect whistleblowers and give a cause of action for retaliation.

In most U.S. states, employment is at-will, meaning that the employer can fire someone for any reason or no reason. It's just that the reason can't be discriminatory or illegal, and that's when people get protected under the statutes. Retaliation is considered a discriminatory activity. So, there has to be some other legitimate business reason that the person got fired, other than making a complaint.

It is important to note that when a workplace investigation starts, it is not uncommon to receive further complaints or allegations—and these may well be cross-complaints. If there is an allegation of sexual harassment, for instance, against the person bringing the initial allegation, that has to be investigated as well. Investigations may well increase in scope as people bring forth different issues about different people.

Avoiding Retaliation

In our hypothetical, Tom and Sally initially felt they could complain to the mission leader about Bill. But that didn't go well for them. And they had no designated person to whom they could take their complaint about the mission leader when they believed she was covering up for Bill.

There should always be at least two designated persons to receive a report, in case one of them is personally involved or is unavailable for some reason. That would have given Tom and Sally a chance to solve the problem without losing their job and then taking it to an attorney. The procedure should contain a guarantee of protection for good faith complaints. This protects people when they complain. (But employees who complain in bad faith—lying, malice, and so on—can be disciplined. The problem here is we don't know if Tom and Sally were acting in good faith in their accusations of the mission leader, because it wasn't investigated.)

Avoiding the Retaliation Lawsuit

How do you avoid a retaliation lawsuit?

First, have an organizational culture that encourages complaints. If you can show that you often receive, and respond well, to complaints, it makes it much less likely that you are retaliating against a given employee.

Second, if you have dealt with the complaint promptly, conducted an investigation, and dealt with any wrongdoing, that helps.

Third, do follow-ups with people who have filed a complaint to make sure there is no retaliation. Ask them on your own initiative if they are being treated okay.

Here are the basic elements for a retaliation lawsuit:

- The employee complained.
- The employer knew that she complained.
- The employee was disciplined or terminated because she complained.

The original complaint doesn't have to have merit. It could be wrong or ill-conceived. It is still going to be difficult to get the retaliation claim dismissed. Sometimes the court will even let a case go forward on just retaliation, after dismissing the original claim.

Now you are going to have to show a non-retaliatory business reason for the termination, so let's hope you had one. And it definitely helps to be able to show why you are firing the employee, such as disciplinary write-ups for the employee's unsatisfactory work or behavior.

You may not have much defense for a retaliation claim if all the employee reviews are positive and you apparently just let the person go out of the blue. Resist the temptation to be overly nice in regular performance reviews and take the time to document all performance deficiencies. If you ever need to answer questions about a termination, whether it is defending against retaliation or an accusation of discrimination, you want objective evidence to back up your decisions.

CHAPTER 2

INVESTIGATION:
YES, NO, OR SORT OF

When a Leader Gets Accused

Everyone's Bible Church has been in operation for about 20 years. Pastor Solid was the founding pastor, though he recently retired. Pastor Friendly got hired as the youth pastor 15 years ago and eventually became pastor of family ministries. He was 25 years old when he joined the church staff. A talented preacher and administrator, Pastor Friendly is also a gifted pastoral counselor and carries a heavy counseling load. Now he is considered by many to be their heir apparent to Pastor Responsible. Some in the congregation enjoy Pastor Friendly's preaching more than the senior pastor's, and he has considerable support from the board of elders.

Pastor Responsible has been preaching a series on sexual harassment and sexual abuse. This is such an important topic these days that he felt the church should be well informed. He assured people that if they had stories they needed to share, the pastoral staff would be available to talk. He expected that perhaps some stories of childhood abuse would come to the surface.

But this week, Pastor Responsible experienced a shock. Mrs. Upright came to him and told him, with sobs, that when she was 20 and in pastoral counseling for depression, Pastor Friendly would give her massages during counseling sessions. Ultimately, he had sex with her on multiple occasions. They were both single at the time. This was nine years ago. She has never told anyone until now, except for her husband, before they got married.

What should Pastor Responsible do next?

The Purposes of an Investigation

Investigations are key to helping an organization gather information about whether harassment or discrimination has occurred and the facts necessary to take appropriate corrective action. Good investigations are part of good member care. They can serve the following useful purposes for your culture and spiritual goals, including these:

1. Give employees confidence that you are caring for them.
2. Root out misconduct.
3. Cultivate a good workplace culture: by taking investigations seriously, the organization creates a culture where voices are heard and unChristlike behavior can be confronted.
4. Encourage support for your moral standards and the standards of conduct for the organization because it sends the message that you take those seriously.

Investigations may protect against legal liability. Taking prompt and thorough corrective action is an affirmative defense to some legal claims, and an investigation can help the organization prove this defense. Even if there is some liability, a good investigation may limit the availability of punitive damages or other liability. On the other hand, a poor investigation could create retaliation claims and liability for the employer. Failure to investigate can also create liability for harm that continues to occur, while doing an investigation may stop further harm from occurring.

When the organization responds to employee grievances by taking them seriously, it creates a culture of truth, where voices are heard and people are not afraid to speak up when misconduct or other unChristlike behavior is occurring. When a problem is identified at the level of an observation or an informal discussion, that is a chance to get it resolved, not to ignore it and let it build up.

What Reports Should Trigger an Investigation

A number of situations call for an investigation. Someone might file a formal complaint or grievance about a topic that would warrant an investigation (sexual harassment, discrimination, illegal behavior). A leader or manager might also hear an informal or casual report or comment—for instance, someone at a party says that another person made an inappropriate sexual comment or engaged in inappropriate physical behavior. Or someone might observe inappropriate conduct. A supervisor may note significant changes in behavior or morale that bear looking into and may uncover something that needs to be investigated. Finally—and one that may leave you wishing you had been proactive sooner—you may get a complaint from an attorney or have a lawsuit filed against you.

If someone in a responsible position in an organization sees or hears something, he is responsible to do something. And if he doesn't do something, the organization can be at fault for his behavior. At the very least, he should pass along the information to the designated persons in

HR who deals with complaints. Unless it is a very low-level employee, knowledge can be imputed to the organization.

Guidance can be obtained from looking at your own internal policies and procedures and determining that a finding may lead to discharge or discipline. Common examples include: employee theft, embezzlement, or fraud; child safety policy violations; and disclosure of confidential information.

Other times, there are allegations of misconduct or discrimination that could lead to liability for the organization if not dealt with promptly: child sexual abuse; sexual harassment; discrimination; failure to accommodate a disability; violation of local laws, and so forth.

One consideration in evaluating your response is the leadership position of the person accused. Misconduct by lower-level employees is easier to deal with and may require less external help.

Decision-makers should consider the chances that the allegations will go public. Anyone who has followed the news lately can see that the chances of abuse allegations hitting social media and the press are extremely high. Listening to and supporting those who may be victims, besides being the right thing to do, is the best way to stay out of the media or not appear unfavorably to the public.

Still, some allegations of misconduct may lead to discipline without reason to conduct a full investigation. In any organization, complained-of behavior may be mild enough that it can be addressed simply. But moral issues that may not have legal baggage but call for discipline can uniquely occur in religious organizations. Some conduct is technically legal and will not lead to liability for the organization, but the organization forbids or does not want to encourage it because of its religious beliefs and requirements that members abide by religious/moral standards. Particularly in the Christian tradition, there may be a greater willingness to confess or discuss this conduct out of a sense of moral/ religious duty than in a secular workplace. For example, discovering a missionary is viewing adult pornography may be problematic from a spiritual perspective, and something a mission would address, but something like that would not typically trigger a response in the secular workplace.

On the other hand, issues like toxic leadership or spiritual abuse, which don't necessarily create legal problems and are not usually investigated in a secular workplace, have a significant impact on an organization's culture. They may be worth investigating formally in a religious organization in order to fulfill the mission of the organization.

Making the Decision about an Investigation

Not all allegations need an investigation. For some complaints, the behavior is easily established. For instance, someone posts a discriminatory comment on social media or says something in front of numerous people. For some complaints, the allegation is so minor that a simple conversation with the alleged offender can both establish and correct the problem. For some complaints, even taken as true, there is no "there" there—what is being complained about is not misconduct or illegal. For most child abuse complaints, the matter should immediately be turned over to Child Protective Services or law enforcement. (We will discuss circumstances where this option is not available or has been tried and has not effectively solved the organization's problem. But the default position is that child abuse must always be reported.)

In order to determine which allegations need to be investigated, you will develop a way to evaluate which claims should be escalated to a full investigation. This involves selecting a decision-maker. Once you have the right decision-maker, that person will evaluate the report to determine if an investigation is needed.

Who ultimately decides whether an investigation should be launched? For less serious complaints, HR may be able to decide. For more serious complaints, it may be top leadership or even the board of directors or elders.

If the person accused is a top leader within the organization, it is important to consider whether anyone in the organization can truly investigate without bias. There may be too much internal pressure or even fears about retaliation. Even if they likely could investigate without bias, would outsiders perceive this to be true? There are serious downsides to an investigation that cannot be accepted as fair.

If you think you need an investigation, there are questions to consider. In light of the allegations, who will be the ideal investigator? A person of the same gender as reporting person? A person of the same or a similar cultural background? Someone inside the organization? Maybe an outside consultant?

Timing of an Investigation

Timing is important. Investigations should generally be begun within days, not weeks or months. Geography may make this a bit more difficult, and how long ago the event occurred can also make investigations more complex, so there will be a case-by-case analysis.

But even with offenses that happened a long time ago, the reporting person will feel slighted and ignored if weeks or months go by and the organization seems to be doing nothing. If it is going to take a while to set up an investigation, for legitimate reasons, it's a good idea to communicate about that with the reporting person or other stakeholders.

Legal Reasons to Conduct an Investigation

An investigation may be legally necessary in some situations. For example, if an employee complains of sexual harassment, you should conduct an investigation of that complaint and take prompt action to remedy any issues. Failure to do so can deprive the organization of a defense in the event of a legal claim, or worse, subject it to legal liability in certain cases. This is particularly true with complaints of sexual harassment, for example.

Even without direct legal liability, when an employer conducts no investigation, it loses the opportunity to learn about bad behavior going on in the organization and might be liable for harm that continues to occur.

Whether or not you think an investigation may be legally necessary, it's a good idea to consult counsel to make sure you are not missing anything—like inadvertent retaliation against an employee.

Policies for Investigations

It helps to have policies that help guide when you should do an investigation. It may be because an offense has been alleged that can lead to immediate discharge or discipline. Other times, it will be misconduct that could lead to liability for the organization if not dealt with promptly (child sexual abuse, sexual harassment, discrimination, violation of local laws, and so on).

Policies can answer questions like the following:

1. How are complaints reported?
2. Who gets notified?
3. When do you notify leadership?
4. Who decides when there should be an investigation?
5. When do you call the attorney?
6. What is the investigative process?

Back to Everyone's Bible Church

Pastor Friendly has assured the senior pastor, Pastor Responsible, that Mrs. Upright is not telling the truth. He did counsel with her, but she was somewhat neurotic, to say the least, and he thought at the time that she might have a crush on him. Though they were both single then, he did not respond to her hints at interest in him, because he didn't feel she would be a suitable wife for a pastor.

"I don't want to speak badly about her," Pastor Friendly said, "but she did have a bit of a reputation with men, if you know what I mean."

Should Pastor Responsible accept Pastor Friendly's assurances that there was no misconduct or should he investigate? After all, he has known Pastor Friendly for years, and he cannot believe something like this could have happened. Besides, he does not think Mrs. Upright will make any further trouble.

Suppose that Pastor Responsible chooses not to investigate. Fast forward five years into the future, and it comes out that Pastor Friendly is accused by multiple victims who are adult women, some of whom were teenage girls from his youth group under age 18. This is started by a former youth group member posting on social media. Other women join in. It hits the press in a big way, because the church ignored the initial allegation when it was reported. And now the church is facing extensive harm with allegations of child sexual abuse.

CHAPTER 3

Structuring the Investigation

An Investigation Gone Wrong

Let's look at a true case involving a "he said-she said" sexual harassment allegation.[1] These facts are drawn from the complaint. Andrea kept receiving unwanted advances from her co-worker, Gray, while at work. He repeatedly asked her out on dates and placed his arm around her whenever he had the chance.

The behavior escalated several months later when Gray sent Andrea a sexually explicit photograph in a text message. She immediately reported the text message to her supervisor, who encouraged her to file a formal complaint. In fact, management suggested that she sit down at a computer that moment and begin the process. So far, so good.

While Andrea was drafting her complaint, Gray walked in to see her crying and typing at the computer. He asked whether she was reporting him, and she avoided engaging in any conversation with him. Gray caught on quickly that he was likely to be in serious trouble for his behavior, and from there he developed a plan. He asked another co-worker to lie about the relationship and tell management that Andrea and he had been in a romantic relationship. He went back into his cell phone and fabricated evidence to make it look like Andrea had been involved with him in a romantic relationship and had also sent him a suggestive photograph. He then printed out screenshots from his phone of the fabricated text messages and had them ready.

The employer approached Gray and confronted him about the allegations. He responded by turning over the printed-out cell phone screenshots he had prepared. Representatives with the employer then circled back to Andrea, informing her they "knew" the truth and had seen proof that it was actually she who engaged in improper conduct. She asked to see the proof, but the employer refused. The employer also refused to look at her cell phone when she offered it to prove that it was really Gray who had sent explicit texts. Apparently without engaging in any further investigation, the employer fired Andrea for engaging in sexual harassment.

What did the employer do wrong here? Let's count the ways:

1. Crediting the alleged offender's accusations/story to the exclusion of all other evidence.

2. Declining to examine contrary evidence tendered by the victim when it knew, or should have known, of the co-worker's retaliatory animus.

3. The alleged offender's accusations formed the sole basis for the employer's decision to terminate.

4. It made credibility determinations without fact-checking or letting Andrea respond.

5. It failed to interview other employees.
6. It ignored extremely relevant evidence by refusing to look at her cell phone.

The Quality of the Investigation

In most cases where a complaint of harassment or discrimination is made, the next step will be to begin an investigation into the allegations and then take appropriate action as a result. [2] A good investigation requires many complex skills that include managing the investigation, conducting interviews, and making credibility determinations. A credibility determination requires the investigative team to analyze the evidence and decide the truth of the matter, sometimes with conflicting statements.

Investigators chosen, whether internally or externally, should have relevant experience and credentials. If the persons involved in doing an investigation do not have sufficient skill, any investigation will not be done well. This could lead to permanent detrimental effects on alleged victims, alleged wrongdoers, and the organization itself. If people realize that the organization investigated poorly, they may lose confidence in the organization's commitment to a healthy workplace.

A poorly executed investigation may also have legal ramifications. For instance, in one case, a company did not follow up by asking the offender about his harassing remarks or check with an employee who had left the company because of sexual harassment. This happened because the investigator was inexperienced.

In a lawsuit, a defendant may sometimes use an affirmative defense, which gives a reason why the defendant is not liable. Here, the company tried to establish the affirmative defense that it exercised reasonable care to prevent or correct the harassment, which is a legitimate defense in employment law cases, but did not succeed because the investigation was so poor.[3]

In another case, the employer weaponized a "secret investigation" into an employee who had reported her supervisor for wrongdoing.[4] Based on the "findings" of that investigation, the employer issued severe and "unnecessary" penalties, which led directly to the employee filing a lawsuit.[5]

When abuse has happened, the religious organization's legal responsibility is determined by whether its actions were reasonable. So, an inadequate investigation of abuse or misconduct may leave an organization open to allegations of negligence. The quality of the investigation may be an important part of the legal defense if there is a lawsuit.

Planning the Investigation

Planning the investigation is important to avoid wasting resources but also to make sure nothing is overlooked. A common but devastating mistake is to talk only to the accused and not to others who could confirm the story. If you have confirmed, for instance, that a youth pastor was kissing a teenage girl, your employment decisions are already simple. However, you may need to investigate to make sure there are no other victims or a widespread problem. Part of planning will be to determine the purpose of the investigation and how you will use the results.

In the planning process, some important initial questions are:

1. What is the investigation seeking to discover?
2. What kind of evidence will be needed?
3. Who will need to be interviewed?
4. Where are the individuals to be interviewed located?
5. Can interviews be done in person?
6. Can any interviews effectively be done over Zoom?
7. What documents need to be reviewed?
8. How will you get the needed documents?

In addition, there are important goals for the investigation that should be addressed in the planning process, so that the organization can do the following:

1. Be objective and avoid bias.
2. Create no further emotional harm.
3. Protect possible victims, including safety for those who may have been harmed and others.
4. Provide justice and due process for possible offenders.
5. Avoid legal liability for the organization.
6. Make findings to a preponderance of the evidence.

Should an Attorney Run the Investigation?

You may choose to have an attorney run the investigation, both for a skill set and for privilege issues (discussed below). Some will argue that if the attorney is giving legal services to the organization, the attorney is not impartial and is biased in favor of the organization. This depends on what the legal services are. If the attorney has been retained to conduct a neutral investigation, find out the truth and position the organization for an appropriate response that cares for those harmed, that is the attorney's task. The attorney should not take on conflicting work with the client, such as litigation defense work.

What Does "Privilege" Mean and How Does It Work?

"Privilege" means you have a legal right to keep something confidential. There are several kinds of privilege, such as attorney-client privilege, doctor-patient privilege, psychologist-patient privilege, clergy-parishioner privilege, and spousal privilege. There are also privacy arguments for personnel files in some states.

A communication that is privileged does not have to be disclosed in a legal proceeding to the opposing side, except in rare circumstances. But if you pass on privileged information to a third party, you destroy (or waive) the privilege. For example, an organization may have various privileged documents. If it hands them over carelessly to investigators who are not working with counsel, these privileges will be waived.[6]

You can set up an investigation in a way that is privileged or in a way that is not. You can always waive privilege later, but you can never "un-waive" the privilege. Some professional teams will work with you to preserve privileges and some will not. If you choose to set up an investigation and waive the privilege, you lose the legal right to keep information confidential.

Why Does the Attorney-Client Privilege Exist?

The purpose of the attorney-client privilege is to encourage clients to be candid and transparent with their attorneys so the attorneys can provide effective representation. Just as physicians need their patients to be forthcoming and transparent about their condition so that they can give effective treatment and prescription, so also attorneys need their clients to be transparent about their problems and legal issues in order to give sound counsel and advocacy. Both physicians and attorneys have duties of confidentiality to those they serve, and both patients and clients have privilege rights to prevent disclosure of the information they give to their practitioners and advice they get from them.

The purpose of the attorney-client privilege is not to conceal information, hide misconduct, or suppress the truth. Indeed, the privilege does not apply to statements made by a client to their lawyer if the statements are proven to a preponderance of the evidence to be made to further or conceal a crime or fraud. Also, the privilege will not apply where someone may be imminently harmed. Moreover, the privilege may be waived by disclosure to a third party.[7]And if the client wants to rely on the attorney's advice as his reason for doing something, he has to waive the privilege. Attorney-client privilege is not some sinister device for evading justice or trampling on the rights of others. Rather, its purpose is to provide space for clients and attorneys to share information and work toward doing the right thing.

Attorneys and their clients need to have protected communications in order to work through difficult problems, including issues related to abuse. An abolition or abridgment of the privilege would have the effect of diminishing accountability and transparency, not encouraging it. The issue is not that outsiders could scrutinize attorney-client communications to make sure they reach whatever standard the outsiders are using for their judgment, which is complicated since the outsiders may not be knowledgeable; but more likely, the communications would simply not be made, and the clients would fail to get good advice.

In light of the attorney-client privilege, churches and ministries can expect that the communications they have with their attorneys will be confidential and protected. But others should not assume that this protection is for the purpose of covering up abuse, whitewashing offenders, or silencing victims. Ministries and their attorneys should use the safe space of communication created by the privilege to engage in candid and transparent discussion of how to properly respond to allegations of abuse.

We Are Taking the Right Actions, So Shouldn't We be Transparent?

Some groups call for transparency with investigations in real time, usually together with waiving attorney-client privilege. In a large investigation that may take a long time, it can be helpful to have regular public updates. However, this is different from revealing everything that is occurring in the investigation. There would be several problems created by revealing all information as it is gathered.

First, sharing information before the investigation is complete and the information is substantiated creates a high risk of unjustly tarnishing someone's character. This might involve someone who has been falsely accused. Or someone has brought a complaint, and others in turn have negative things to say about that person. Until evidence is substantiated, people should not have their reputations ruined.

Second, if someone has had negative material revealed about them, they also have a potential legal claim for defamation. So that makes the organization more likely to face liability for doing an investigation.

Third, even if the investigators are able to substantiate information, this is only to the standard of "more likely than not." It may not be reasonable or just to ruin someone's reputation for a 55 percent chance they have done something wrong, for instance. This is one reason that employment investigations have historically been confidential.

Fourth, it is almost impossible to keep an investigation on track if the investigators are being actively critiqued as they work. Often, such critiques come from persons who are not neutral, impartial, or knowledgeable about the professional task at hand. Interested persons share and discuss information that supports their own angle or agenda, as they have no professional duty to be neutral and unbiased. That is distracting and upsetting for investigators. While investigators are supposed to be neutral and impartial, active attacks on them make it difficult to remain so and may create secondary trauma.

Information about the investigation that gets passed around (nowadays, usually on the Internet) tends to be misunderstood, confused, and garbled. People share information they do not have personal knowledge about. Much public discussion about investigations ends up being "mostly false."

Fifth, even if you think you have done everything right, a plaintiff's attorney will not agree with you. A transparent investigation will be reviewed in great detail, looking for any possible error—and there is no such thing as a perfect investigation.

In addition, a plaintiff's attorney will use all discoverable materials not just to support a single lawsuit, but also to explore and see if there are any other potential lawsuits against the organization. Once the privileges are waived, a plaintiff's attorney can go after all privileged documents for decades.

The best practice norm is that investigations are kept internal to the organization and as confidential as possible until the investigation is complete.

What Does a Good Investigation Look Like?

Besides achieving a reliable result, a good investigation needs to be defensible to the general public or at a trial. A good investigation should include the following:

1. The investigation should take place reasonably promptly (how promptly depends on the gravity and urgency of the situation).
2. Important witnesses should be interviewed.
3. The team must assess credibility and consider whether there is corroborating evidence.
4. Records, files, and notes must be preserved or destroyed in accordance with sound principles. (We will discuss this further in chapter 8.)
5. The investigator should have no personal stake in the outcome or close personal relationships with witnesses.
6. Steps taken in the investigation should be documented.
7. Attorney supervision and documentation should be adequate to preserve the privileges.

How Broad Should the Investigation Be?

The organization's first duty is to protect those who have been harmed, and its second duty is to protect the organization. The investigation should be just broad enough to do both for a given situation, and no broader. Unnecessarily broad investigations do not necessarily help victims, are likely to damage the organization, and are likely to be fantastically expensive. They take so much time that the organization's appropriate response is badly delayed. Looking at everything can mean addressing nothing.

Another reason that the investigation should not be broader than necessary is that everything in the investigation may potentially come out in litigation. Counsel or experienced human resources staff will help you set tight time frames, limit the scope of the investigation, and limit the documents made available to the team. The investigation can be broadened carefully as needed.

To be clear, this does not mean concealing misconduct, hiding documents, or failing to interview important witnesses. There are times when a narrow, focused approach is needed, and other times when investigators must dig deeply into the files or the history of the organization.

General Investigative Process

Depending on the severity of the allegations, running an investigation may be quick or lengthy, simple or complex. Here are the overall steps for planning purposes:

1. Receive the complaint. The individual receiving the complaint will take down the initial story, which may be in written form or relayed verbally. Observed behavior can also trigger an investigation, such as if a supervisor witnesses inappropriate behavior. This has usually already happened by the time you start planning, though not always.

2. Appoint an investigator. This may be someone from HR or may be an outside third party. We'll talk more later

about internal versus external investigations. But for now, understand that this choice will depend on several things, such as how serious the allegations are and whether they involve senior leadership. The investigator must have the ability to be truly independent, and the investigation must legitimately appear to those involved as truly independent, which are related but not identical concepts.

3. Gather and review documents. There may be emails or other documents relevant to the allegations.

4. Conduct investigative interviews. The investigator will conduct interviews with the reporting person and any other relevant individuals who might have information. The investigator will also talk to the person accused for his or her side of the story.

5. Reach findings and conclusions. After the investigator has gathered all the information, he or she will use that information to reach findings and decide what is more likely than not to have happened in any given scenario and whether this conduct violated organizational policy or standards.

Some organizations have HR handle abuse investigations, and some assign persons with special training and responsibilities. Either is fine, as long as personnel are trained in investigations and protocols for conducting investigations in a way that preserves the rights of both alleged victims and alleged offenders.

Notifications and Insurance

For almost all investigations, you will want to notify and involve HR and some level of leadership, perhaps including leadership at a high level. Depending on the severity of the allegations, you will also want to notify your insurer. If there is a lawsuit or administrative charge or threat of other legal action, the insurer should certainly be notified at this point.

How much can you tell the insurer? Some courts have held that communication with the insurer is privileged. Other courts have held that their interests are not aligned. It depends partly on the jurisdiction and also on whether or not there is litigation yet. Your counsel, your insurer, or both, should be able to tell you whether the communications are privileged in your state for how far the matter has progressed. Don't overcommunicate with your insurer until this analysis is in place.

An Example of a Leadership Misconduct Allegation

Rev. Dr. Important's former assistant, Connie Complainer, comes forward and says that he had an affair with her. The board of elders is informed. Rev. Dr. Important hotly denies this allegation and assures the board he has done nothing wrong, giving a plausible explanation.

The board members are torn as to how to proceed. They realize that normally allegations like this are investigated. But they have always had confidence that Rev. Dr. Important is a godly man. They do not want an outside investigation, as it will be expensive and potentially embarrassing. They ask Sam Faithful, one of the board members, to investigate. He talks to Connie and hears her story. He then talks to Rev. Dr. Important, who of course denies Connie's claims.

Another board member, Timmie Tech, suggests that Sam review all email communications between Connie and Rev. Dr. Important. Sam asks for these communications and is told by Rev. Dr. Important that those emails are gone. He suggests that perhaps they didn't get retained when the computer systems were updated.

Sam concludes that there is no evidence of wrongdoing. Things go on as usual for a few years—until a messy moral explosion reveals that not only did Rev. Dr. Important have an affair with Connie but also acted immorally with several other women.

If an organization has allegations brought against a leader similar to our fictional Rev. Dr. Important, how should it respond? Will there be a serious investigation? Will the standards for moral and spiritual behavior be equally applied to a leader? Will the organization be serious about protecting its weaker members and living out its spiritual values?

If a ministry regards allegations of misconduct as serious, it will take steps to investigate and provide spiritual care. Unfortunately, there have been a number of cases where the organization's leader (like Rev. Dr. Important) was believed and there was no investigation—only to have a messy moral explosion several years later.

Consider also that someone who takes Christian leadership seriously should want to model appropriate behavior. Some accused leaders will call for an investigation and voluntarily step down for a time. They are modeling care for their organization. It should raise concern when a leader tries to manipulate the situation to avoid being investigated, as this is likely a form of institutional betrayal.

Additional Structures for Large Investigations

Some investigations are large and complex in structure, and may take a considerable amount of time. They may benefit by some or all of the following additional components.

Planning Committee
In a large, historical review, there might be incidents that were thoroughly dealt with at the time, and others that were not. Complaints might be quite serious; others could be less so and may not warrant revisiting decades later. Part of the investigative planning is determining the scope of the investigation with reference to what is in the files.

One helpful approach for this is to set up a planning committee that is independent from the investigation. It could include the investigative coordinator, if there is one, a lead investigator, and one or more independent consultants who are knowledgeable about historical investigations and child abuse (or other abuse being considered). For impartiality, it is best to gather information from the organization ahead of time, but not have the organization represented on the planning committee.

Coordinator Role

In large investigations that will last a long time, a coordinator role can be helpful. Separate from the lead investigator, the coordinator is responsible for putting together a team, giving any needed training to the team, communicating with the organization, gathering documents and having them indexed, managing or monitoring logistics, and supervising the conclusion of the investigation.

The coordinator typically does not conduct interviews or make factual findings, while the investigative team does not directly communicate with the organization. This distance helps to prevent bias in making factual findings, which is more of a potential concern when long-term relationships develop. The coordinator does not make findings or draft the Master Report but may draft a public report or statements of findings provided to the persons who have made reports or been accused.

Review Panel

Another helpful structural approach for large investigations is to create a review panel. This is a group of independent experts in the subject matter (usually child abuse), who take on a confidential role of reviewing the Master Report and making recommendations about actions to take. This could range from disciplinary actions against offenders or leaders to restorative actions for survivors. Again, having external recommendations helps the board be advised confidentially from the perspective of an outsider on how best to handle matters.

Survivor Coordinator

In some large investigations, it can help to have a representative of the group of concerned individuals, such as survivors, work together with the coordinator. The survivor coordinator can raise questions and concerns from survivors, assist in tracking people down, help to provide updates, and generally improve communications in a lengthy investigation. The survivor coordinator can, if appropriate, also do presentations to the investigative team or review panel, helping to present the survivors' perspectives.

Public and Private Updates

For lengthy and extensive investigations, or where there is an active survivors' group, it can help reassure all concerned if there is a public-facing website that gives information about the investigation and regular updates. Examples can be seen at teliosinvestigations.com/investigations. This can also be a place to publish any public reports after the investigation.

Even if a public-facing website is not needed, participants in the investigation may benefit from detailed information about what is going on, depending on their level of uncertainty or anxiety. This can be provided in formal communications ahead of interviews, during interviews, or in response to questions as asked. Be aware that some persons will seek to exert pressure and make demands on the investigation. To the extent that the requests can be accommodated for people who may be experiencing trauma, they should be. To the extent that they are demands that would erode best practices in the investigation, the investigator should politely explain why she cannot comply.

CHAPTER 4

CHILD ABUSE ALLEGATIONS: SPECIAL CONSIDERATIONS

How Child Abuse Allegations Can Be Complex

Cindy Reporter is a seven-year-old who attends EBC with her family. One day, her mother and father came to talk to Pastor Responsible. They told him that Cindy had reported that Tim Childer had taken her to a closet in the church and molested her. Tim is a 15-year-old boy, who is fairly meek and quiet.

Pastor Responsible reported the alleged abuse to the city's Child Protective Services. CPS started an investigation. Although Mrs. Reporter insisted that Cindy had been molested, in a child forensic interview, Cindy denied that Tim had done anything. She just said that they had been in the closet. CPS did not pursue the matter further.

Pastor Responsible held a church meeting, letting people know that there was an allegation that a child had been touched. He did not provide Tim's name, because Tim is also a minor and because the allegations had not been substantiated. The church provided information to help parents talk to their children and see if there had been any other incidents. No one came forward with other incidents.

Mrs. Reporter continued to talk to and question Cindy about the situation. After a period of time, Cindy started to relate details of the alleged molesting.

Mrs. Reporter went back to Pastor Responsible. She was very angry that Tim was still allowed to attend the church, insisting that the leaders make his name public. Mrs. Reporter felt that Cindy had confirmed the abuse. She decided to tell as many people as she could herself. People started to treat Tim differently, and soon he developed an anxiety disorder.

Evaluate Mandatory Reporting

Organizations that work with children should have policies for reporting child abuse. Reports received should be funneled to the child safety coordinator or similar designated person.

Supposing there has been an allegation of child endangerment or child abuse, decision-makers should evaluate it quickly. Is it a matter of brief neglect of a child, a boundary violation such as putting a child on one's lap, or child sexual abuse? Most state statutes require reporting on a "reasonable suspicion" of abuse or some similar standard. The ministry should be aware of who is legally a mandatory reporter, but may also have a policy to report whether or not it is mandatory.

If a report should be made and is not made promptly, there may be criminal penalties for not reporting. Some states provide very short timelines. There could also be civil liability for not reporting. A report may be required even if the abuse is not directly connected to the organization, such as suspected abuse within a family associated with the organization (a family attending a church, for instance).

If the alleged victim is now an adult, it may still be appropriate or wise to report. A report may be required in some jurisdictions, depending on mandatory reporting laws. Or in the alternative, the organization may support the victim in making a report. Even if reporting seems optional, it's extremely important to consider whether children may still be at risk. If they are, action should be taken to protect them. Determining the best approach may require some legal analysis.

Allegations of relatively minor behavior are simpler to deal with. If they do not rise to the level of child abuse under the facts known, a mandatory report may not be needed. However, the allegations should still be vigorously addressed. Violating boundaries or ignoring child safety are red flags for abusers, and those who will not cooperate with child safety standards should be promptly dismissed or kept from working with children.

Clergy-Parishioner Confidentiality

Some churches have set up confidential communications of a pastoral nature, which remain confidential under a privilege. The confessional is the best-known example, but in many cases either state statutes or common law protect from disclosure communications between parishioners and clergy that are intended to provide a safe place for the care of the soul, including wrestling with serious sin. When and whether this privilege applies depends on the doctrine of the particular church, but it may prevent a mandatory report from being made.

Minister and clergy should be careful before entering discussions to determine if the privilege may apply and to be sure that the person sharing information also understands if it applies.

In churches where it does apply, a priest or minister should make significant efforts to have the offender self-report.

Child Safety Plan

Once there has been an abuse allegation, for the limited purposes of child safety, you must assume the allegation is true. This means that the child in question and any other children who could be at risk must be protected. The alleged offender must have no further access to children until an investigation, either by law enforcement or within the organization, has revealed that there is not a safety risk. A child safety plan should be created.

A child safety plan may involve creating temporary living arrangements, such as removing an alleged offender from the household (if the alleged offender is a minor, then one of the parents may need to leave the household with him). The plan may also include administrative leave or other working arrangements. It may require notifications within a need-to-know circle. It may involve counseling or other services for the child who has been harmed. But the organization cannot afford to wait weeks or months for investigative results before ensuring child safety.

Relying on Government Investigations—or Not

Once a mandatory child abuse report is made, the ministry may be able to rely on law enforcement or CPS investigations, at least for determining whether child abuse happened. If there is a law enforcement investigation, the ministry should not interfere with it.

Sometimes the government investigation does not produce a useful result for the ministry. Some possibilities are:

1. Law enforcement or CPS drops the investigation, determining that they do not want to file charges, either because they do not think abuse happened or because they think they will not be able to prove it beyond a reasonable doubt (a much higher standards than employment investigations).

2. Agencies won't share any information, even as time goes by. It can be hard to access the information law enforcement is gathering.
3. Agencies will not take jurisdiction in the first place, because of when it happened (perhaps too long ago), because it did not happen in their jurisdiction, or because allegations are too minor. This leaves the organization on its own.
4. The child abuse piece was dealt with, but the organization needs more information to make ministry employment or discipline decisions.

In these cases, you may need a partial or entire investigation sponsored by the organization. Perhaps all of the situation needs to be investigated, including whether abuse happened, or only a portion, such as whether leaders responded adequately to abuse. In addition, it can be helpful to have psychological evaluations done—a trauma evaluation for alleged victims and a forensic psychological evaluation for alleged offenders. This gives guidance both for organizational steps to ensure safety of children and care for those involved.

Even if law enforcement is investigating, it will likely be necessary to have a child safety plan and response plan. How will you keep safe not only children who may have been harmed but also *all* children? How will children who may have been harmed be cared for? A plan can be developed to identify children who may have been harmed and help them.

Child Abuse Investigations Versus HR Investigations

Conceptually, a child abuse investigation is a subset of an employee or HR investigation. It focuses both on a particular type of wrongdoing and a wrong done to someone who is not an employee. The overall legal standards and best practices for an investigation are quite similar.

However, personnel involved should also have particular training in child abuse response protocols.

If an organization has to investigate child abuse (or has to talk to a child for some other reason), it should use a child forensic interviewer who is trained to talk with children. Without a skilled interviewer, there is great danger of getting a completely inadequate or inaccurate response from a child—and even causing the child to believe things that are not true with leading questions.

Child Safety Notifications within the Church or Ministry

In addition to reporting to authorities, there may be other appropriate notifications, both within the organization (such as to leadership or the crisis response team) or to other relevant persons such as parents (making sure first that they have legal custody). It is unlikely that law enforcement or child protective services is going to do broad notifications, so it will be up to the organization to determine if other children have been harmed.

Use great caution when making such an announcement. First, it is not appropriate to share the names or details about minors, even if they are the alleged offender. Likewise, it is not appropriate to share the names of alleged victims, because it can add to their trauma.

In many cases, it is not appropriate to share the name of the alleged offender, regardless of age. Just because there is an allegation does not mean it is true. Identifying the person could destroy his reputation and career even if he is innocent. There may be exceptions, such as where charges have been filed, where the abuse is admitted, or where at least a "clear and convincing" standard of evidence has been met. But in most cases, identifying the alleged offender should wait until after law enforcement actions are complete or an investigation has made a determination.

In the United States, churches and ministries have the right to discuss decisions regarding their own internal affairs in what is called a "qualified privilege." This right is strong as it relates to church or ministry members and becomes weaker as it gets close to making a matter generally public. There may also be defenses related to discussing matters of safety and public interest.

The best approach is for an organization to limit sharing information to members or long-time attendees, be careful to limit information to known facts, to give as little information as needed to protect children, and to be restrained in comments about the alleged offender.

For example, a church could hold a meeting to inform members and parents of attending children that there has been a reported allegation of child abuse. The church could say whether the allegations are current, whether other children are thought to be at risk, and possibly the age range and gender of children who might be at risk. Then it could provide some guidance to parents on how to talk to their children about whether they have experienced any inappropriate contact.

Once there have been charges filed or public releases of information, the organization can provide more detailed information.

CHAPTER 5

BUILDING THE
INVESTIGATIVE TEAM

A Poor Investigative Team

Sam Spade's investigative business has been growing, and he has more work than he can handle. He asks his brother, Steve Spade, to join him. Steve is quite different from Sam. He spent his youth as a star athlete rather than reading detective literature. Sam gives Steve some basic orientation and sets him to work investigating allegations out of the past. At first, all seems to go well.

But a couple of months later, Sam receives a complaint from the client. He discovers that Steve has been conducting phone interviews rather than traveling to meet with people in person. Sam listens to a recording of the interviews and finds that Steve's interview technique leaves much to be desired. He talks too much and tends to ask leading questions. And Steve has written up a report concluding that the accused is guilty—but he never interviewed the accused. What is Sam to do? Start by firing Steve, for sure.

Who Should Be the Point Person from the Organization?

It helps to have one point person in the organization responsible for coordinating the investigation and working with the lead investigator, whether the investigation is run internally or by an outside investigator. This can be the head of HR or in-house counsel, or perhaps outside general counsel.

Should the Investigative Team Be Internal or External?

You may need an internal or an external investigative team, or even a mixture of both. Whether the investigative team is internal or external depends on a variety of factors, including the seriousness of the allegations, parties involved, investigative skills available to the organization, extent of the potential liability, and the position of the accused within the organization.

This decision depends on evaluating skills, possible liability for the organization, and potential bias in the investigation. Bias easily creeps in. Hiring an independent investigator to conduct the interviews, evaluate credibility, and make findings can help an employer be responsible during an investigation. An outside firm not only avoids the appearance of impropriety and bias, but also may limit the possibility that decision-makers will be manipulated by people they work with and not make the right decisions.

This may be more important if there are high-level liability concerns. For instance, if top-level leadership has been accused, it is quite difficult to run an internal investigation adequately. Having an outside team helps avoid allegations of bias and ensure the investigation is run well. Outside investigations are more costly but may be needed for both PR and liability purposes.

Consider the following points in structuring an internal or external investigation:

1. Ideally, two people should conduct the interviews, so there must be trained people available.
2. Important interviews should be done in-person if at all possible.
3. Interviewers may need special skills, such as understanding disabilities, child forensic interviewing, or other languages and cultures.
4. Sometimes a mix of internal and external resources can be used.
5. Investigators should not be involved as a witness, or be biased, or even have the appearance of being biased. For example, the investigative firm cannot have close ties to a plaintiff's injury law firm that is involved with alleged victims in the matter.
6. In-house counsel or the HR director may be involved in the investigation but should not be if he or she has made underlying decisions about the matter or is directly accountable to the person accused.

An internal team understands the organization and can maintain control of the investigation, but the members may not be objective and may lack experience. They may also be under pressure to ignore problems or resolve matters too quickly.

An external team is better insulated from pressure or allegations of bias but lacks the deep knowledge of the organizational environment. In addition, external team qualifications and positions should be reviewed to make sure they do not have inherent biases. For instance, a victims' advocacy group would likely make a good consultant but a poor investigator.

Attorney Versus Private Investigator?

Pros and cons should be evaluated when considering whether to use an attorney, a private investigator, or a mix of both. Ultimately, what is important is skill set, experience, and talent. Some private investigators are much better than some attorneys, and vice versa.

Pros and Cons of an Attorney Investigator

An attorney's investigation can be attorney-client privileged.

Often, work product from an attorney investigation is of higher quality and will be more compliant with legal standards.

An attorney may have experience in a particular area of law, such as employment legal standards.

An attorney may or may not have extensive interviewing experience.

An attorney cannot interview represented persons without their attorney present.

An investigation performed by an attorney is usually more expensive. Sometimes it is considerably more expensive, though sometimes the difference is mitigated if the attorney generates work product more quickly.

Pros and Cons of a Private Investigator

Investigators may be more expert than attorneys at actual interviews unless the attorney has extensive experience.

If a private investigator is used, none of the material will be privileged unless the investigator is hired by the attorney or is instructed by the organization to work at the attorney's direction. For minor investigations, it may not matter if the investigation is privileged, but this could become an important issue if the organization is likely to come under serious attack.

A private investigator should have experience in the legal areas at issue. For example, some investigators have experience with child abuse (or other crimes) but not with workplace employment situations (such as sexual harassment or retaliation). It is not uncommon for private investigator-written reports to create legal problems for the organization. This can be addressed by partnering with an attorney with expertise in the area.

Potential problems for private investigators include licensing issues. In many states, there are criminal penalties for doing private investigation without being licensed. In other states, licensing is optional or voluntary. In some states, an investigator working directly for a lawyer is exempt. Sometimes in-house investigators are exempt. An investigator might be able to work on a single case at an attorney's direction but not to do further work in the jurisdiction.

The licensing problem should be carefully considered on a case-by-case basis. Possible approaches are to define roles appropriately, to work through a law firm, or to hire a local licensed P.I. as an advisor and backup. In most overseas jurisdictions, a U.S. investigator can investigate for a U.S. organization, but it would be worth checking with local counsel.

Contracting with an Outside Investigator

The organization should have an engagement letter with any kind of outside investigator. The letter should define the scope of the issue to be investigated and what the approach will be if the scope grows. The letter should establish the investigator as fact-finder. If the investigator is an attorney, it should define at least generally what legal advice will be provided.

The parties should agree whether the investigator will or will not make recommendations for action or remedial measures. It is generally best for investigators not to make recommendations, or at most only oral recommendations. Written recommendations infringe upon the authority of the organization's leaders or board and can create further liability if the organization chooses not to follow the advice (and it is likely discoverable). Some investigators insist upon being able to make recommendations, sometimes publicly. Consider carefully whether to hire that investigator.

The engagement letter should address confidentiality and privilege issues and specify the person to whom the investigator reports. It should address what will happen to materials generated by the investigation, such as who retains them and for how long. It should address whether the investigator is permitted to make any of the findings public or will generate a public report. (See the section describing different ways of handling public reports.)

The letter should address the investigator's role in any post-investigation litigation and how that will be paid for. It should also address whether the organization will indemnify the investigator in case the investigator is sued for taking part in the investigation.

There should be clarity for the investigator as to the mechanics of the investigation, such as where interviews will take place, how remote witnesses will be interviewed, and how witnesses are scheduled. The investigator should discuss what kind of confidentiality or *Upjohn* warnings[1] are given to witnesses, particularly if the investigator is an attorney. The investigator should know and agree with the organization's position on recording of witness interviews, whatever that is.

The format of the final report to be provided should be clear, including whether it is oral or written, and how detailed.

Criteria for an Investigative Team

Organizations often use internal personnel. Sometimes they hire one or more outside investigators, either to join the team or run the investigation. Other times they retain an attorney.

Consider the following possible needs of the investigation:

1. Do the people who will investigate (internal or external) have

sufficient experience and training to cope with the problem presented?

2. Does the team share the values of the organization?

3. Are secondary areas of needed knowledge available, such as medical background, psychological training in sexual abuse, expertise in interviewing alleged offenders, or experience in interviewing children?

4. Do interviewers have the languages required, and is translation available?

5. Do persons have legal knowledge of the subject area, such as relevant employment law or information about child abuse?

6. Is there someone on the team who has sufficient understanding of the organization's structure and theology?

7. Do persons have a good working knowledge of evidentiary standards and credibility issues like recovered memory or social contamination?

8. Is the proposed team sufficiently impartial so that it will not in fact be biased one way or the other, and will not give the appearance of bias if the investigation is later challenged?

9. Can the team legally do what it proposes to do? Do the persons involved have the necessary credentials and licensing? This is necessary both so that the investigation is legal, and so that it is credible if it is ever challenged.

10. Is the team properly advised (and willing to agree) about issues such as privilege and who makes final decisions?

11. Is the team willing to observe confidentiality?

12. Is the team willing to act at the direction of the attorney, if that is proposed? (Some investigators will not act at the direction of an attorney.)

13. Does the team have the time and resources to conduct the investigation promptly and thoroughly?

14. Is the team dynamic such that people can work together

effectively, given the geographic and communication issues frequently present in an investigation?

15. Does the team understand careful and thorough recordkeeping in light of potential litigation?
16. Are persons on the team good communicators, and will they be good witnesses if there is litigation?
17. Will they be able to generate a complete and accurate report?

Even setting up an investigative team is a complex task that may require expert advice.

CHAPTER 6

INVESTIGATION IN PROGRESS

An Inadequate Investigation

A female teacher said she was sexually harassed by students at a Catholic boys' high school.[1] The teacher taught biology and also was involved in campus ministry. The all-boys school had a long history of sexual harassment of women teachers, including taking up-skirt photos, leaving graphic cell phone messages, making threatening phone calls, and other inappropriate actions. These actions involved the plaintiff and other female teachers.

The teacher complained that the school did not investigate sufficiently, including that it did not:

1. Contact police promptly enough.
2. Seriously address offensive and sexually graphic graffiti.

3. Deal sufficiently with student sexual references on social media (it made them take down references and suspended them but did not determine if offensive language was widespread).
4. Sufficiently question or examine students related to the up-skirt photos incident (specifically, allowing or encouraging students to delete photos or deny having photos and failing to order a forensic electronic investigation).
5. Adequately investigate an up-skirt photo competition among students.

The school disciplined some students, but the question was whether it really dealt with widespread harassment. An expert report highlighted problems with investigations, including:
1. Violations of confidentiality.
2. Not properly interviewing witnesses.
3. Failing to corroborate allegations.
4. Failing to perceive patterns of misconduct.
5. Interviewing students over the phone.
6. Failing to remember crucial details of the investigation.

In some ways, doing investigations wrong is worse than not even doing them at all. In this case, the greatest liability for the school was created by the improper investigation, not by the underlying problem. Investigations should comply with best practices.

Conducting Interviews

It is best to work with two interviewers, so one person can focus on asking questions and listening while another takes detailed notes. They both may be present in person, or one can join by videoconference. Another advantage is that having two interviewers provides a chaperon when interviewer and witness are not the same sex.

The investigator will give an introduction to set ground rules and explain the purpose of the interview to the witness in somewhat general terms, giving away no information about what he or she might (or might not) know, and showing no pre-judgments. For example: "I asked you to meet with me because I am investigating a claim about [workplace misconduct] and I need to ask you and some others about that." There is usually no need to explain to a witness how they were selected.

The investigator can share how confidentiality will be handled and confirm the importance and requirement of full and complete answers, getting the witness's commitment to provide those. It can also help to share the standard of review (usually preponderance) for determining factual findings in the investigation.

If an attorney is doing the interviews, it is important to be clear who the client is (the organization), especially when interviewing leaders (the *Upjohn* warning).

At the end of an interview, the investigator will likely ask if the witness has anything to add or anything else that the investigator should know.

Detailed notes should include date, time, and names of all individuals present.

Being Clear on Different Kinds of Conversations

People who have suffered various types of abuse often find it difficult to speak about the experience. Trauma from abuse almost always has a significant impact on people. It can be years before they are able to come forward. When they do come forward, they may have hopes and expectations for how their stories are received. Unfortunately, there is often confusion about the types of conversations that might occur and how these can vary.

When someone comes forward in a ministry or employment setting with a story of abuse, the story should be received with compassion and respect. In this context, the story should be treated initially as if it is true. The employer will then take next steps to gather information. If the account is of child abuse, a report to the authorities will typically be triggered by "reasonable suspicion," which is a fairly low level of credibility. It would be inappropriate for someone initially receiving the story to show skepticism about it.

When someone speaks to her therapist about abuse, she can expect a compassionate response to the revealed experience and a shared goal of therapeutic healing. The therapist's job is not to evaluate the credibility of the account or the probability that particular facts are true, but to help with the healing process.

When someone tells a story to a victim's advocacy group, the recipient will generally assume that the story is true. Their mission is to stop abuse and advocate better ways to respond to it. Their goal is not to test the truth of individual stories.

An investigation takes a different approach to truth. An investigation is intended to be neutral and impartial. If an investigator is asked to receive a survivor's story without challenging it and without skepticism, the proper response is to clarify that this methodology is not possible. The job of an investigator is to seek the truth and evaluate credibility, not to assume it. Having presuppositions that a story is true—or not true—could jeopardize the impartiality of the investigation.

It may be wise to explain to people being interviewed about accounts of abuse that it is not the job of the investigator to provide therapeutic support to an individual. They may need to bring a support person or make an appointment to see their spiritual advisor or counselor after the interview.

Trauma-Informed Approaches to Interviews

Although investigators cannot assume the truth of the account that a witness brings forward, they can use trauma-informed approaches to interviews. To reduce anxiety, it is good to have clear communication ahead of time about what will happen. As mentioned above, it may be wise to allow witnesses to bring someone for support, as long as that person agrees not to interrupt or add to the dialogue.

Early in the interview, the investigator can explain the interview process and ask if there are questions. The witness should be assured that she can ask for a break if needed. Having bottled water, coffee, and tissues available is helpful.

Questions should generally be open-ended, allowing the person room to tell his story in his own words. Follow-up questions can address details and elicit explanations but should not be presented in a challenging or hostile way. The investigator can be firm but gentle and sensitive in demeanor.

If a witness seems upset during the interview, the investigator can pause and give her space, perhaps even asking if a short break is needed. If a witness seems to be having trouble, the investigator can ask if she needs to end the interview.

At the conclusion, or if the interview has to be ended early, it may be appropriate to ask if the witness has a care plan in place, will be safe driving, or needs additional help. If it appears that a witness is in danger, a 911 call may be necessary as a last resort.

Sequence of Interviews

Typically, investigators will interview the reporting party, people who may be victims, the accused, and any other witnesses to the events or people who may have information about the allegations. This may include former employees.

The following order is suggested for interviewing:
1. Reporting party and people who may be victims.
2. Other witnesses who may have insight.
3. Accused.

4. Other witnesses suggested by the accused.
5. Circle back to initial witnesses as needed.

Sometimes it is not possible to follow this order, due to timing of trips or witness cooperation. But if possible, it is best for allegations to be gathered first, then the accused has a chance to respond.

Interviewing a Reporting Person

The reporting person should be interviewed early, usually first, and it is important for the assigned investigator to reach out to this individual. The reporting person can usually provide the names of follow-up witnesses, which can aid in the investigation.

The reporting person often is the one who has been harmed, but not always. If the reporting person is someone other than the one harmed, that person should likely also be interviewed as early as possible. This helps set the facts for the investigation and gives the investigator a basis for determining who else to interview and what other information is important.

Particularly where investigative topics may be private or embarrassing matters—like sexual harassment—it is preferable to have the interviewer be of the same gender as the reporting party.

If the reporting person has completed a written complaint, it is useful to go over that with them line by line. The investigator will also want to ask open-ended questions and obtain a narrative response before moving to questions about specific details, such as the number of times something has occurred. The investigator will want to find out if the person has made a complaint before, and what the person knows personally versus through hearsay.

The investigator may ask if the person has documents or records, such as emails, voicemails, texts, or photos that relate to the incidents at hand. The investigator will likely ask if anyone else has experienced similar treatment or if there is anyone who might be a witness.

While the person's story may be quite emotional, and the investigator may convey empathy, it is important not to signal belief or disbelief.

Interviewing a Child

If a CPS or law enforcement investigation ensues, do not interview children until these agencies have completed their investigation. Consider whether it is necessary to interview a child or whether you can get needed information in some other way. Children should not be interviewed without their parents' consent, so it may not be possible to interview a child.

If, for whatever reason, you need to interview a child, use a child forensic interviewer. CPS, or perhaps a therapist, may be able to advise on how to locate a trained professional who will work privately. If someone who is not properly trained interviews a child, the child's recollection can be contaminated. An incompetent interviewer can actually create false memories in children by leading and other types of inappropriate questions.

Parents should also not interview their children because of similar risks. In one case, allegations of inappropriate behavior by another minor could not be pursued because zealous parents had significantly contaminated the testimony by repeated and inappropriate questioning.

Interviewing a Person Accused

A person accused, whose career and life as they know it is often on the line, is entitled to a fair process. Unlike criminal process, there is no assumption of innocence, but there should not be an assumption of guilt either. Fairness or "due process" is essential.

Don't be surprised if the interview turns out to be somewhat hostile. For anyone, facing allegations is highly emotional. Realize that the accused is undergoing pain and trauma, whether or not the allegations are true.

An alleged offender will often be informed ahead of time that there has been an allegation, though not given details. Providing details is a matter of discretion. Sometimes it is best to surprise the alleged offender, such as when the questioning is to be about details of alleged sexual harassment. But at other times, it is best to give more time for the person to prepare for the interview, such as when questions may focus on the contents of organizational documents. This depends on the nature of the allegations and the overall situation.

If the alleged offender does know of the allegations ahead of time, it is important to be sure this person understands that he or she must not retaliate against others or try to manipulate their testimony.

At the interview, the alleged offender should be informed generally that a complaint has been made, such as, "We are here to discuss concerns about whether you have complied with our child safety standards." If possible, the investigator should go through the complaint detail by detail to get the reaction of the accused.

If the alleged offender wishes to bring counsel or another support person, it is best to allow it. In fact, if the person has counsel, the interview cannot be conducted either by an attorney or at the direction of an attorney without allowing the person's counsel to be present, because of attorney ethical rules.

The accused should be asked about the relationship with the reporting party or those who may have been harmed. This can help to clarify the allegations.

The investigator will let the individual do most of the talking. It is best not to offer information to the person being interviewed without careful thought about whether it is necessary or appropriate to do so. Instead, ask open-ended questions and let the individual tell his or her side of the story.

The investigator can ask if there are other witnesses to talk to or if the accused can provide relevant documents. Again, the investigator should not signal belief or disbelief of the accused's story.

In interviewing a potential wrongdoer, it is especially important to make sure he knows the material may not be kept confidential, and that if an attorney is involved, any privilege belongs to the organization and not to the individual.

Sometimes issues of confidentiality or requirements of anonymity may mean that not all details of an accusation can be shared with the accused. However, it is important that enough details be shared that the accused can give a fair response. If this is not the case, you may not be able to substantiate because of due process problems.

If the decision about the alleged offender is to take disciplinary action, some kind of appeal process is helpful both for fairness to the person and for defending the decision later.

If you engage a third party to investigate workplace misconduct, it could be considered a report that would normally come under the federal Fair Credit Reporting Act. Another statute, the federal Fair and Accurate Credit Transactions Act (FACTA), provides an exception to the FCRA for an investigation related to misconduct, as long as the communication is only provided to the employer or an agent of the employer.[2] But if the employer is going to take any adverse action based on the communication, the employer is required to give the employee a summary of the nature and substance of the communication. The requirements of FACTA may limit what can be shared with other organizations, such as sending churches, so you may need to seek counsel on this. Also, be aware that some states may have more stringent standards.

Interviewing Collateral Witnesses

Talking to collateral witnesses is an important part of the interview. Investigators will give less detail to these witnesses about the allegations. It is best to try getting answers to open-ended questions rather than offering detail.

Witnesses can be asked about specific incidents they witnessed, and also who else would have information. Often, they can help identify former employees who may have useful information.

Allowing Third Parties to Be Present

While it is preferable to not have third parties present at an interview, it is sometimes necessary. If a witness is represented by counsel, and an attorney is conducting the interview, the witness' attorney must be allowed to be present. Sometimes a witness will refuse to talk without an attorney present, and in these cases, the organization should also be represented.

In other situations, such as if someone is a minor or has special needs, a parent or guardian should be allowed to be present. If a person has been traumatized or has psychological needs, having the individual's counselor present can protect everyone involved.

In an employment situation, employees don't generally have a right to have a third party present, unless they are union representatives. [3]

In general, if someone strongly desires a support person, it is better to allow that to happen than to create a power disparity or an uncomfortable situation.

The role of the third person must be clear. This individual should agree to attend as a silent presence, resisting the urge to offer their opinions in the interview. If the individual is an attorney, he or she should understand that it is not a deposition and the attorney should not participate actively. A support person should not be someone who will also need to be interviewed. However, she can be interviewed first before serving as a support person.

Conducting Interviews Remotely

Often people wonder whether investigations can be done over Zoom or another videoconference service because it is much more convenient and meeting in person places a burden on key witnesses. In-person interviews remain an industry best practice, especially for key witnesses. For collateral witnesses, especially where there are no credibility issues, remote interviews are possible. Also, an option is to have the second interviewer present by videoconference. This can save considerably on the cost of the investigation.

Investigators are not simply recording witnesses' words in order to preserve them. They have the responsibility to determine both whether witnesses' statements are true and whether they believe it to be true (which is not always the same thing). They are not just listening and taking notes; they are weighing what the witness has to say and gauging the person's credibility. This is a difficult task, and investigators need every tool at their disposal. Virtual platforms such as Zoom do not allow them to fully see or hear the interviewee. Thus, a virtual interview limits their ability to perform the task.

The interviewee's body language from his feet to his hands and head is important. The person's ability to see the investigator is important too. Some witnesses will change their position in mid-conversation if they determine from the listener's body language that their story is not having an effect. Saying the words out loud and observing the effect on the listener is important to both sides of the conversation. It guides both the witness and the interviewer in the direction of truth.

Physical presence is also valuable in evaluating credibility. Some people sweat and show other physical signs of being anxious when they are not telling the truth. Some people may be able to sit still and stare at a camera when lying, but their legs under the table may be shaking. Some people have a difficult time looking another person directly in the eye when saying something that is not completely true. Unobstructed eye contact is extremely important in gauging credibility.

But it is literally impossible to look someone in the eye during a virtual interview. Each participant looks at a screen, not even a camera, and their mind subconsciously is aware of this and feels much more at ease. Eyes naturally wander around the screen during a virtual call rather than looking directly at the person, which would be the natural tendency in a normal face-to-face conversation. It's generally not possible to line up the camera perfectly with the face, so no one is ever really looking directly at the other person.

Suppose an investigator wrote a report stating that during a virtual interview, the witness displayed a shaking body, profuse sweating, a quivering voice, and lack of eye contact. How would an outside observer respond? The response might be: "There's no way you could clearly see or hear any of that in a virtual interview." Or, "You couldn't possibly see the person's entire body language." Or, "The person could not possibly look the interviewer in the eye because it was a Zoom call." In other words, physical observations from a virtual interview are easy to discredit. And observations about body language that are imperfect can lead to the conclusion that the interview process was unfair to that witness.

Sometimes witnesses want to provide only a written statement. It's much easier for someone to articulate their position on paper than to say it face-to-face. This is not a good idea, for the same reasons an in-person interview is important.

Both the person bringing allegations and the person being accused deserve a completely fair process—which means they are not only entitled to an in-person interview with a full hearing, but they are entitled that the person disagreeing with their position also be tested with an in-person interview.

What if Someone Refuses to Cooperate with the Investigation?

An employer has an obligation under certain circumstances to conduct the investigation, even if the reporting employee, for example, does not want an investigation. The employer should generally have a policy that failure to participate in an investigation may be grounds for discipline, up to and including termination. Without such a policy, it may be hard to get people to cooperate.

However, be wary of enforcing this policy on a reporting party or someone who may have been harmed. If the person has been harmed and does not want to talk, you can increase his or her trauma by applying pressure. Also, employers can invite big trouble for retaliating against reporting parties, and forcing someone to participate in an interview could cross that line. Reporting persons are in a different position than accused persons, so they should be given some leeway.

An accused person can usually be required to participate. If an employee attempts to resign rather than participate, consider whether the organization should accept the resignation or should insist on participation. If the alleged behavior is less egregious, resignation may be fine. If it is extremely serious, such as sexual assault or child abuse, the organization may refuse to accept a resignation. Obviously, you cannot prevent someone from resigning or walking out, but this is a question of how the incident is framed in personnel records and references. The point is that refusing to participate in an investigation can itself be subject to disciplinary action.

Even if an accused person does not have to participate and chooses not to participate, investigators can take this into account. For one thing, if an accused does not participate, allegations go without rebuttal by him. This makes it more likely that allegations are substantiated. In general, if someone does not participate, inferences can also be drawn about credibility or how supportive the person is of the values of the organization.

Confidentiality in the Investigation on Both Sides

Confidentiality in employment investigations is tricky. In an employment setting, it is important *not* to promise confidentiality to witnesses for information they provide because it is a promise you are unlikely to be able to keep. In broader settings, investigations may be set up with confidentiality as an option, which we'll discuss in more detail.

Sometimes organizations are tempted to tell everyone interviewed to keep the matter totally confidential by not sharing with others. This isn't a good idea, as the National Labor Relations Board frowns on blanket confidentiality requirements. Instead, analyze confidentiality on a case-by-case basis and determine whether to ask for witness confidentiality for one of these four reasons:

1. Protecting witnesses.
2. Preventing destruction of evidence.
3. Preserving testimony and thwarting false testimony.
4. Preventing a cover-up.

Document your reasons before requiring or requesting confidentiality. It is likely reasonable to ask people to keep information about the investigation confidential while it is going on. When witnesses talk to each other about an ongoing investigation, it can create significant social contamination of testimony.

In asking for confidentiality, investigators can make clear that they are not trying to shut down a witness's ability to share or process her own story, as this can be very traumatizing. Specifically, you want confidentiality for the investigative interview and would prefer that people not discuss the investigation.

If the witness needs to talk to someone to process the interview, a confidential relationship with a spiritual advisor, counselor, or someone in a similar role offers an appropriate course of action. You don't want to leave someone in a position of feeling harmed by the investigation.

Be aware that it is extremely difficult to enforce confidentiality on witnesses. If they are employees, it is possible but risky. If they are not employees, it is impossible. Some witnesses may even go on social media after an interview to express indignation that they were asked to keep confidentiality, alleging that the request amounts to a cover-up.

In requesting confidentiality, watch for evasive non-responses, such as, "Well, I can't lie if someone asks me a question."

If witnesses resist the idea of confidentiality, the investigator will know to be extremely careful about providing any details. And if a witness does violate confidentiality, that may lead the investigator to make appropriate judgments about the witness's character, credibility, and motivation.

Religious doctrine may have something to say about how employees should behave during these investigations, and it may be appropriate to talk to witnesses about biblical reasons for confidentiality. Discouragement of gossip, judgment, reputational concerns, and other religious facets may rightly come into play.[4]

Anonymity in the Investigation

Anonymity considerations are definitely a complicating factor in investigations. Sometimes organizations receive anonymous tips, and there is not much anyone can do about that. If there is enough factual evidence, the tip can be followed up, and if there is not, it cannot be acted upon.

In employment settings, employees should be informed that reports cannot necessarily be kept confidential. Employers have an obligation to follow up. In the case of a child abuse report, the report must be made. A person receiving the report must be sure to make this clear. If a religious organization has a clergy confidential privilege (such as a confessional privilege), those conversations should be clearly established before receiving information.

In some investigations, it is possible to offer either partial or complete anonymity. In large investigations, sometimes survivors and other witnesses wish to have their name kept from the organization. This is done by coding their names in the version of the Master Report provided to the organization. Another level of anonymity may come if the witness wants to be completely anonymous to all other witnesses.

Anonymity also has certain implications. If a person has brought forward allegations of abuse or is a witness to abuse, investigators can follow up on these allegations more effectively if they can openly share the person's name during the investigation. If they cannot recount certain factual circumstances to others, especially to those accused, it is unlikely that they can substantiate or corroborate them. If a person chooses to remain anonymous, it will likely affect the investigators' ability to uncover information and properly follow through with the allegations. However, the information can be used as background information.

Also, requests for anonymity do not shelter what other people may say about a witness or information that may exist in documents. For instance, if a non-anonymous witness brings up the name of an individual who has requested anonymity, the non-anonymous witness's statement is not confidential. Therefore, the name of the anonymous individual in this context is not confidential. The function of anonymity is to keep confidential the person's identity as a witness and what they have said, not their existence or circumstances as described by others.

Some people are not eligible for anonymity, such as those accused of wrongdoing and being investigated. Also, individuals sometimes choose to make statements of facts or accusations on public forums like Twitter or Facebook. Public statements are not confidential. Suppose an individual, whether a witness or not and whether anonymity has been requested or not, makes public posts. That person is subject to have their posts included in the report and be evaluated for credibility just as any non-anonymous witness.

Giving Updates on Progress of an Investigation

Reporting persons have the right to know that the organization is investigating promptly and thoroughly. Let them know that you are taking the complaint seriously and have begun your investigation.

But the reporting person doesn't get a full report on what everyone said or have the right to see the investigative notes. In the U.S.

employment context, investigations are confidential. Under General Data Protection Regulation (GDPR)[5] and similar laws, people cannot see the personal information of other people.

Standard of Review to Reach a Conclusion

Most internal investigations use a standard called "preponderance of the evidence," which means that the investigator is looking for whether it is more likely than not that the misconduct happened as alleged. Effectively, this gets past the 50 percent mark.

This is a different and much lower standard than the "beyond a reasonable doubt" that is the most common criminal justice standard.

Because of the lower standards of evidence, there is much less certainty in the results than with a criminal trial. If there is a finding to a 60 percent chance, for instance, there is still a 40 percent chance that the allegation is not true. And if there is a finding of 30 percent, there will be no substantiation, but still a 30 percent chance that the allegation is true.

Because of this, employment investigations have typically been kept confidential. The certainty is sufficient to make an employment decision, but not sufficient to put a person's name out publicly. There is a risk of doing an injustice, and also of a defamation lawsuit.

There is also a child safety issue to be considered. If there is no substantiation but still some significant chance that abuse happened, the organization may want to make, not a disciplinary decision, but a child safety decision, keeping the person away from children in the ministry.

Red Flags and Common Mistakes for Investigations

No investigation is perfect and all investigators make mistakes in every investigation. That said, good investigators will constantly seek to improve, whether through self-evaluation, continued reading, having their techniques audited, or getting feedback from those present. There are common mistakes and problems worth keeping in mind.

Failing to plan can cause problems with the investigation:

1. It can lead to overlooking important information or important witnesses.
2. It can lead to spending unnecessary resources on an investigation that is too broad.

New investigators should partner with more experienced ones to learn, as investigative inexperience can cause problems:

1. Good investigative techniques are based on training and experience.
2. Investigators may be experienced generally but not experienced in a particular type of investigation.
3. They may not be aware of all relevant legal standards or may misinterpret what they are hearing.

Common mistakes in questioning are:

1. Asking leading questions rather than open-ended ones (even more dangerous when interviewing children).
2. Not following up on questions where more information has been indicated.
3. Talking too much rather than listening.
4. Revealing too much to a witness.
5. Failing to take adequate notes.

During the investigation, there are some things to watch for:

1. The appearance of lying or destroying evidence should trigger further investigation of the individuals who have done (or may have done) that.

2. As you interview, if there is good indication that some others might have useful information, they should be interviewed, especially in cases that allege widespread wrongdoing.
3. Handle confidentiality issues carefully.

Investigators should set up interviews properly:
4. Avoid phone or Zoom interviews, particularly for important witnesses. Investigators will want to be careful not to let initial screening calls get out of control and turn into interviews.
5. Make sure the environment is comfortable and adequately chaperoned by the second investigator.
6. Make sure there is an adequate amount of time for each interview.

Outside consultants or experts may be needed:
1. Where electronic data is involved, use professional forensic analysis. Local law enforcement may be able to recommend someone.
2. For specialized interviews, such as with children, used trained interviewers, such as a child forensic interviewer.
3. For psychological issues or witnesses who may decompensate (have a collapse), seek psychological advice and consider having an interviewer with psychological expertise. It may be necessary to have a witness's counselor present or have an opinion in writing from the counselor that the witness can safely interview.

A common mistake is having a goal to prove (or disprove) the allegations. Any lack of objectivity or bias can cause huge problems. It can even make the entire organization liable for an adverse employment action or lawsuit.

Additional Review

Once the interviews are complete, there may be some wrap-up work. After the interviews, the investigators may request and review additional documents or do follow-up interviews if necessary. They may circle back to complaining party or other witnesses for an additional interview if necessary to have a complete investigation.

CHAPTER 7

MEMORY AND CREDIBILITY ISSUES

Memory and credibility issues can muddy the results of an investigation. Witness credibility depends on a number of factors and should be evaluated carefully.

Memory conformity and misinformation are also important concepts. Misinformation generally refers to the phenomenon that post-event information, whether in the form of questioning or discussions with others, can affect memory and later recounting of an event. A recovered memory is of an event (usually abuse) that the person did not remember for a long time but has come to remember.

Truth, Lies, Facts, and Issues

Molly Missions always said she had a happy childhood as a missionary kid. Sure, she suffered from the usual third-culture kid issues, and she sometimes had conflict with her dad. But Molly told people it was a good way to grow up.

Then as a young adult, she went into counseling for an eating disorder. Around the same time, she was involved with an online missionary-kid forum where her peers began to share about abuse.

During counseling, Molly started to recover memories of her father raping her. Then she recovered memories of her brother raping her, her brother's friends raping her, her uncle raping her, and African men from their church raping her. As these memories returned, Molly was an emotional wreck. Eventually, she was diagnosed with Dissociative Identity Disorder.

Molly has now reported her abuse to her family's mission agency, which has begun an investigation. Molly's family denies that any of this abuse ever happened. There is no question that Molly is suffering greatly. How does the investigation evaluate her credibility? How would investigators know if these memories were factual?

Assessing Credibility

Assessing credibility is an important part of interviewing. Investigators will evaluate credibility by considering whether:

1. The witness was telling the truth or had reason not to tell the truth.
2. The witness has a personal interest in the outcome.
3. The witness remembers well or has memory issues or had memory issues.
4. The witness had the opportunity and ability to observe things firsthand.
5. The witness understood the questions.
6. The witness or the testimony was corroborated or contradicted.

In considering plausibility, investigators can consider which witnesses' stories make the most sense. If one person's version of events defies logic or common sense, it may not be true. Could the witness have heard or seen what he or she claims? Should she have heard or seen things that she did not admit to?

For any witness, it is important whether the person had firsthand knowledge and saw or heard events directly, or was told secondhand. Both can be valuable, but the distinction is important.

Investigators will evaluate whether statements are specific and supported by evidence or whether they are vague. For example, if someone claims there has been "spiritual abuse" but cannot give any specific examples, that reduces the credibility of the allegations. "Lots of people think so" or "Lots of people are unhappy," is not evidence but is put forward as evidence surprisingly often.

Investigators will consider the accused's version of the story. Does the person deny it outright? Or explain it in some way? Perhaps there was a misunderstanding. Or perhaps one side or the other was exaggerating. Then it becomes important if there are witnesses or documents that support or contradict a person's statement.

Self-contradictions are also important, whether major or minor. The person's story may not have stayed consistent through questioning.

Investigators will also evaluate how witnesses act. For those accused, the response to the complaint can be important. Are they genuinely upset or dismissive, or do they show no reaction? Does an accused person deny something categorically or perhaps give an ambiguous statement such as, "I don't remember anything like that." Offenders will often admit to more minor behavior or deny remembering something or otherwise respond in oblique ways.

It may be important to evaluate what information gets left out. If someone omits an important detail, or admits to it only after being confronted, that is significant.

Prior behavior can also be important. Perhaps an accused person has faced prior similar complaints. Or perhaps a reporting party has a habit of making complaints. Perhaps there are other incidents between individuals or an important history in the relationship. Loyalties and grudges can provide motives to lie, exaggerate, or deny stories.

Social Contagion or Memory Conformity

One subset of memory change is social contagion theory, or memory conformity theory, which looks at the effect of social interactions with others on memory and reporting. Social contagion theory refers to the spread of a memory from one person to another by means of social interaction, including conversational interactions.[1] In some instances, the speaker can impose a new memory onto the listener, that is, a memory of something that the listener did not experience. In other instances, a speaker imposes on the listener an alternative rendering of something that the listener experienced. This contagion or contamination can also occur during an investigative interview, if it is done improperly—the investigator can influence the witness's memory.

Memory conformity, on the other hand, refers to instances in which two people talk about a past event, and what one person says can influence what the other person reports about the event.

Some Research and Case Studies Around Memory

Many studies have shown that people can be led to believe they experienced events, when in fact, they did not.[2] People have been led to believe that they were born left-handed, that they broke a window with their hand, or that they got lost before age three.

As an example, let's take a look at some of the details surrounding the Oklahoma City bombing.[3] When Timothy McVeigh arrived at Elliot's Body Shop to rent the truck used in the explosion, CCTV showed that he arrived alone. When questioned after the explosion, the owner of the shop, who showed McVeigh the truck, and the secretary, who dealt with the paperwork, did not remember anyone with McVeigh. However, a mechanic, who saw part of the interaction between McVeigh and the secretary, recalled an accomplice with McVeigh. After speaking with his coworkers, his report led the owner and the secretary to report that McVeigh was not alone and, on the basis of their statements, the FBI began a massive hunt for John Doe 2. The FBI now believes that the mechanic was recalling a different customer and that his false memory of an accomplice spread to the other people's memory. Remembering traumatic events incorrectly is not surprising, as traumatic memories may be more disorganized. [4]

Eyewitnesses can influence each other's memories for an event by discussing what happened.[5] In conducting a study on memory influence, pairs of participants were chosen, and each were separately shown a video of the same event, with each video containing unique items only seen by one witness. Essentially, it was the same scene from two different perspectives. The witnesses were told they were seeing the same video.

In one perspective, a girl can be viewed stealing ten dollars. In the other video, she cannot. Participants then discussed what they saw with their partner before performing a recall test. As a result, 71 percent of witnesses who had discussed an event with a co-witness reported items of information that they had not seen but had acquired during the course of the discussion.

Notably, the study measured whether the discussion with the co-witness would affect the other's perception of guilt and whether a crime had been committed. For example, only one vantage point was able to see the girl in the video commit a crime; but 60 percent of all participants who had not seen this vantage point came to believe she was guilty after discussing the event with a co-witness who had seen her commit a crime. In other words, discussion with a co-witness who believed in the guilt of the subject of the film was enough to convince the majority of participants that she was a thief. This study proved that participants who discuss the event with a co-witness will incorporate critical (unseen) details into their memory reports, even when asked to recall only that which they have seen themselves.

This phenomenon is not just limited to witnessed events either.

Simply hearing the very early memories of others can alter one's own autobiographical memories.[6] Another study consisted of 200 participants describing their earliest memories. Before doing so, approximately half were exposed to colleagues who described very early memories such as their first step or second birthday. Participants who had been exposed to the colleagues produced memories that were a year younger on average than the memories reported by the controls.

The results of the study indicate that autobiographical memories for early events are quite susceptible to influence. Social information can influence autobiographical memories even when the form of influence is indirect. The results of the study suggest that individuals who listen to others share their own memories in a context such as group therapy may be influenced by the stories and take parts of these memories as their own. Social influence may have different effects on individuals, from changing details in a memory to the creation of entirely false memories.

This also suggests that people who discuss organizational situations in online settings may have a similar experience of memory conformity. While it is understandable that people want to share and process their situations, it can have implications for the reliability of testimony in an investigation.

According to another study, relationships between co-witnesses enhance susceptibility to misinformation.[7] This study built on the memory conformity study done by Lorraine Hope and colleagues in 2003 to see whether prior acquaintance with a co-witness would affect memory conformity. Researchers divided 96 participants into pairs and asked the subjects to view an event (from two different perspectives). Then the subjects were to discuss the witnessed event with a stranger, romantic partner, or friend. One person saw a theft take place during the event. The pairs discussed the events and then took a recall test separately.

Results indicated, in line with previous research, that all co-witness dyads were susceptible to misinformation from a co-witness. However, previously acquainted witnesses were significantly more likely to incorporate information obtained solely from their co-witness into their own accounts. Participants in a friend or couple co-witnessing dyad were more likely to assert that the target took money from a wallet following discussions with a co-witness who had viewed a theft (even though they themselves had not seen that particular scene). The study demonstrated that previously acquainted co-witnesses produce less accurate individual accounts than both non-acquainted co-witnesses and witnesses who do not discuss the incident with anybody else. Friend groups who discuss events may take the truth of others' memories for granted and may be less able to make clear distinctions between what they personally did and did not see.

One study dug deeper and discovered that in a group setting, people tend to believe the first person who remembers an event and may be more likely to incorporate those stories into their own memories.[8] The study sought to examine the effect on memory of the assumption by group members that the first person to introduce a particular topic is more accurate. Participants were shown 50 pictures, and then shown a video of two other participants (colleagues) giving responses to whether the pictures had been presented. This was followed by a recall test.

In the majority of cases, participants believed the first speaker to be more accurate and more confident than a subsequent speaker. Participants were more likely to report as their own memory what the first speaker reported than what a subsequent speaker reported. The study showed that the response order effect was not due to some intrinsic characteristic of what the first person had to say.

A 2007 study revealed that people can be implicitly pressured into forming false memories by social interactions.[9] Participants studied lists created by researchers to elicit false memories and then worked with virtual partners (included in the study) on a recognition memory task. During the group tests, the participants were pressured to recognize words that did not appear on the list. The participants then engaged in individual recall tests. The study concluded that people are more likely to incorporate incorrect information into their own memory reports when there is social pressure to do so, rather when merely exposed to incorrect information.

The results of the study suggest that increasing the level of social pressure to respond in a particular manner will often increase the likelihood that a participant will mimic associated responses on group tests. The study was also consistent with previous research findings demonstrating that the likelihood that participants will incorporate misleading information into their own memory reports is dependent on the plausibility of the misleading information.

Alcohol and drug use can also affect memory (including legitimate drug use).[10]

Forgetting and Remembering Abuse

It is not uncommon for people to repress traumatic memories. According to one study, 38 percent of women later forgot sexual abuse that had been reported 17 years earlier. This was more likely when they were very young and the perpetrator was someone they knew.[11] However, these lost memories can be revived, and sometimes repressed memories of traumatic events do resurface in people's minds.

It is therapeutically improper to attempt to uncover or to validate recovered memories. Being encouraged to retrieve memories will produce additional memories, but there is no evidence those memories are accurate.

Even experienced clinicians cannot tell if a report is true or is the result of a memory being implanted in someone's mind by one of the various methods described in the previous section. Convincing pseudo-memories can be constructed. In one case, a man recovered memories during EMDR therapy about his Holocaust experience in a concentration camp. However, his date of birth confirmed that he was not old enough to have been there.

One may be tempted to believe that if a person recalls a memory multiple times and reports it the same way that this means it must be true. But repeatedly recalling memories is not evidence of increasing validity. Somatic, or body memories, may be real expressions of trauma but cannot be assumed to correlate with visual memories.

For a recovered memory, the investigator cannot assume either that the memory is true or false. It could be either. Without additional corroboration, an investigator cannot accurately substantiate a recovered memory.

Implications for Investigators

Investigators must keep memory issues in mind when conducting interviews as part of an investigation. Any steps the investigation can take to minimize external influences on a the memory of a witness or interviewee should be taken. A person's memory can be altered and false memories created simply by discussing events and accounts with others. This could include discussing it with co-witnesses but also in therapy contexts. Studies also show that discussing events with friends is more likely to influence memories than with strangers.

Interviews should be conducted with only one interviewee at a time. If spouses or others are interviewed together, they may easily contaminate each others' memories.

If it is possible to keep witnesses from discussing the situation with each other, that is for the best. If witnesses will not agree to keep interviews confidential and are discussing events widely in an online group, that should at least be identified as a possible contaminating factor. Such an online group is a likely breeding ground for memory distortion.

The investigator should not think of the investigation as trying to prove that something did or didn't happen, but rather to simply determine what the evidence suggests happened. Leading questions should be avoided and open-ended questions asked as much as possible.

The investigator should be wary of testimony that may be tainted by false memories. If witnesses have discussed an event with one another, then the investigator should take great care not to give undue weight to the consistency of their independent statements when judging their accuracy. The independent statements may have become consistent because of the previous discussion. Finding out whether or not witnesses have previously discussed the event may be important to an investigator's determination of credibility.

To determine the consistency of memories, investigators should, to the best of their abilities, determine if memories have always been remembered. Were events previously reported? To whom? Can those persons be interviewed to confirm the report?

Particularly for recovered memories, investigators should determine if there is any other corroboration, such as other victims with the same story, a confession, or a very early report of the incident.

In many studies, researchers worked toward figuring out whether someone's memory was based on something they had seen or experienced themselves or was based on something they had been told by a companion. Researchers would ask questions like "Do you remember?" instead of "Do you know?" to try to pin down where the memory came from.

An investigator can use questions like, "Have you talked to anyone about what you have told me today? How many times?" Or, "Have you written about it on social media? Have you read accounts from others on Facebook or other social media?" With the passage of time, witnesses may not be able to identify where their accounts originated. But it could be useful to ask some of these questions.

When interviewing someone who had an experience as a child, investigators must consider when the memory was encoded and the age of retrieval. While the person may be an adult now, this is a child's memory and not an adult's memory. Thus, investigators should consider whether the child was old enough to form the temporal aspects of the memory (with seven or eight or older being more likely to be accurate than younger ages). Freely recalled information is more likely to be accurate than information retrieved in response to prompts.

Investigators may wish to employ certain questions to (roughly) assess subjective memory with older adults. These questions could include: "Do you have any difficulty with your memory? Do you forget where you have left things more than you used to? Do you forget the names of close friends and relatives? Have you been in your town and neighborhood and forgotten your way?" Such questions may help determine the reliability of the interviewee's memory.

Credibility Matrix

It can be helpful to obtain information on whether a witness is credible and has a reputation for truthfulness. This has long been considered important evidence in our legal system. For instance, in trials, while prior acts cannot generally be brought into evidence, witnesses can comment on a person's reputation for truthfulness under Evidence Rule 608.

The approach is simple. Investigators create a list of witnesses, those who might be witnesses, those involved in some way, and perhaps some other irrelevant names. Witnesses are asked if they know each other and then asked to gauge the credibility of others. An introduction is given somewhat like the following:

> This last segment of the interview is about credibility. I am going to list a series of persons and for each person I name, I would like you to give me your assessment of that person's credibility on a scale from 1–5, with 1 being you can hardly believe anything they tell you, and 5 being you can trust anything they say as the truth.

The reason I am asking is that I am trying to get an accurate understanding of how credible each person is. The credibility ratings that you provide will not be shared with anyone. All we do is aggregate the data from everyone's responses to determine each potential witness' average credibility rating. For each person I name, you can feel free just to state a number or to give commentary explaining the rating you gave them. You should also be aware that not all these persons may be witnesses or involved in the investigation in any way.

At this point, some witnesses might ask for clarification as to what specifically the questioner means by "credibility." The most common distinction is between credibility in terms of reliability (credibility of one's statements of future intent and doing what they say they will do) and credibility in terms of truthfulness (veracity of one's declarative statements of historical facts). Generally, we are inquiring into the latter sense of credibility.

In some instances, a witness will assert that he or she does not know a person well enough to accurately judge their credibility. In such cases, the witness should not evaluate that person. The best practice is to simply have a blank response from that witness as to the person in question. There may also be variation in caveats, disclaimers, and qualifications that a witness might provide along with their assessment of an individual's credibility. For example, a witness may candidly state a strong personal bias toward or against the individual. While the numerical responses are the only data that can mathematically figure into the aggregation, any commentary a witness makes in conjunction with providing a response should also be noted as it may discount or otherwise affect the import of the witness's response for an individual.

If there are witnesses who have sought complete anonymity as to their testimony, investigators must consider whether it would violate anonymity to put them into the list. It may be better to omit them. If there are strong concerns in the investigation about witness identification, this credibility matrix may not be a useful technique.

Investigators will then aggregate the data and put it into a chart. Often, a simple average is sufficient. If it is an investigation that is highly polarized, with people "taking sides," it may be necessary to balance out the number of people opining on each "side." In addition, if someone's responses obviously reflect their personal biases, rather than an objective evaluation or credibility, that says something about their objectivity and believability as a witness. We sometimes get responses like, "They don't agree with me so they are a 2."

Investigators should realize that the credibility matrix is practical rather than scientific and should only be used to supplement their own credibility observations and other data. It should also be used cautiously. For instance, in one major investigation with people taking strong "sides," the credibility aggregation was not really useful, but witnesses' responses were useful in evaluating whether they were objective or biased witnesses.

CHAPTER 8

HANDLING THE INVESTIGATION DOCUMENTS

Testing Investigative Limits

Ricky Reckless, the HR director of World All Over, a large international nonprofit, comes to Alice Attorney to talk about an investigation they are doing. Ricky explains that Hans Handsome has been accused by Vickie Victim of sexual harassment. Ricky and Alice need to obtain documents for the investigation, and the CEO told Ricky to make sure that doing so is legitimate.

"What about searching through Hans's work emails?" Ricky asks Alice. "After all, Vickie says that he harassed her on work email."

Alice agrees that might be acceptable, depending on the ministry's privacy policy about employee email and computers. It would also depend on what jurisdiction Hans works in, because European privacy laws are more stringent than those in the U.S. Some legal analysis may be necessary.

Ricky suggests approaching a friend of Hans's to get access to his private Facebook page. Alice recommends against that, because of possible privacy violations. Hans has not given Ricky or other leaders from World All Over access to his Facebook page.

Ricky found a Post-It note on Hans's computer that has his Gmail password. Would it be okay to log into Hans's Gmail? Or in the alternative, what if Hans has Gmail set to automatically log in when you open the browser?

"No," Alice says. "World All Over cannot access an employee's private emails."

Lastly, Ricky has heard that Hans does not have his phone password protected. Would it be okay to sneak a quick look at his text messages while he is in the bathroom?

"Definitely not," says Alice. "If Vickie wants to share messages from her phone, that is up to her, but stay out of Hans's phone."

This hypothetical—and we hope unlikely—scenario points to the challenges and limitations in gathering information necessary for a thorough investigation. Inexperienced and perhaps overzealous members of an investigative team may want to go beyond the proper (and sometimes legal) boundaries for data collection.

The methods used to gather information and the types of documents obtained weigh heavily in the determining the fairness and clarity of an investigation. This chapter provides guidance for the documents that should be procured and the appropriate handling of these documents.

Preliminary Review of Relevant Documents

Since gathering documents is an important step in an investigation, which ones should be sought? These include:

1. Ministry codes of conduct or doctrinal statements.
2. Child safety policies, disciplinary policies, or other relevant policies.
3. Personnel records, including disciplinary actions or prior complaints, for both the alleged victim and accused.
4. Previous complaints in other formats.
5. Employment handbook.
6. Releases for cell phone, electronic device, and computer records.
7. Relevant electronic records.
8. Records of the initial allegations or other statements.
9. Any employment contracts or acknowledgments to abide by policies pertaining to those involved (if not in personnel file).
10. Internal correspondence regarding the complaint.
11. Any video, audio, or voicemails regarding the events in question.
12. Relevant emails, texts or other electronic communications.
13. Any papers filed with state administrative agencies, EEOC, union grievance, and so forth.
14. Previously prepared statements by any witnesses.
15. Any notes of previous meetings with any party.

The investigative team will gather policies, documentation, a written complaint, or other similar records. It's important to identify the relevant rules or policies that may have been violated. Here are questions the investigators may ask in interviews:

1. Was the policy in writing?
2. Was the accused or the complaining party aware of these rules or policies?
3. How was the policy communicated, and when?
4. Has there been discipline in the past related to these policies?

Limitations on Employer Document Searches

Employers have certain rights to search for documents within the organization. Most employees of private organizations have limited rights to privacy in their work computer and other documents, depending in part on whether there is workplace policy in place stating that they don't have privacy. The laws of the country can also affect how much privacy employees have, sometimes limiting employer rights by statute. Some courts have recognized a legal cause of action called "intrusion upon seclusion," based in common law privacy rights, if an employer invades an employee's privacy to an extreme degree.

Here are guidelines for employer searches for documents:

1. The search should be rationally related to a legitimate need of the employer.
2. Prior communication of the search policy to employees and applicants is desirable.
3. Intrusiveness of the search is limited to the minimum needed to meet legitimate need of the employer.
4. Employee consent can be express or implied, but should be formally obtained whenever possible.
5. Searches should be uniformly or randomly enforced (no discriminatory implementation).
6. The search should provide adequate safeguards for protecting employee privacy.
7. Search results should only be provided to those who need to know.

Issues may also arise when an employer desires to monitor an employee's business phone, email, or otherwise conduct surveillance. Intercepting communications over the telephone raises particularly tricky legal issues under federal law or the law of other countries, so this must be addressed on a case-by-case basis with counsel.

Be aware that the law governing these employer searches varies from country to country, so you may need to check local legal standards.

Document Retention Policies

All organizations generate massive amounts of data. Document retention policies establish how long documents and emails are kept, and when they will be destroyed. Some documents should be kept forever (board minutes, insurance policies), but others can be destroyed. The key is to maintain consistent policies.

When every document has been saved forever, investigations and litigation can be massively expensive because of the cost of sifting through everything. It is much easier if previously implemented document retention policies have limited the materials to be searched.

With respect to all abuse issues, documents such as complaints, investigative files, and reports should be saved indefinitely. Formerly, statutes of limitations meant that an organization would not face litigation after a particular period of time, but this concept has eroded. Decades from now, it may be asked what you knew and how you responded to a particular problem.

With reference to a particular issue, you may not continue to destroy data according to your regular policy when there is anticipated litigation, because of the "litigation hold" that requires you to preserve it.

How Does Data Protection Affect a Cross-Border Investigation?

Data privacy laws vary greatly between countries. For instance, E.U. data privacy directives contain protections for personal data that are much stronger than those applying in much of the U.S., though certain states are also passing stringent laws. If you are investigating in the E.U., you may need a detailed analysis of the law in the jurisdiction as it interacts with your network structure. How will you collect and review documents? Can you export them outside the jurisdiction? Are you aware of local rules about making audio recordings?

You may have to obtain consent from employees, redact personal information, or review the information without exporting it.

Some countries have very strict laws about conducting internal investigations and use of information, and employees may not need to cooperate with an investigation. Examples: France has a blocking statute that limits investigations and use of information; China has a State Secrets Act.

Local data protection rules may need to be evaluated for the investigation, so that the organization doesn't wind up breaking laws.

Confidentiality in Personnel Files

In most jurisdictions, employees have access to their personnel files. Except for the official short Statement of Findings that is released to the parties involved, results of the investigations (such as a full Master Report) should not go in the personnel file but should be kept separately and confidentially.

Different jurisdictions may have different approaches to this, and counsel for the jurisdiction may need to be consulted. In areas where data protection laws require release of this information to the individual concerned, there may be an exception to producing documents that contain the personal information of others.

Advantages and Disadvantages of Recording Interviews

Usually, attorneys do not record interviews, but sometimes other investigators do so. There are advantages of recording interviews:

1. They provide a permanent, accurate record of the interview that other team members can listen to. When investigations

take place over a wide geographical spread and witnesses are hard to contact, this can be especially helpful.

2. They provide an opportunity to evaluate interviews done by less experienced investigators and redo them if necessary.

3. When recordings are so easy to do, it may be hard to justify not doing them.

There are also disadvantages of recording interviews:

1. The organization will likely have to produce recordings or share them with the person interviewed.

2. Witnesses often feel uncomfortable and may give less information if they know they are being recorded.

3. The recording does not reflect body language.

4. The recording can be used to pick apart the written report, as there will always be arguable inaccuracies and subjective statements. It may be preferable to have just a written report and let challengers state what they believe should be added.

5. Recording someone's statement gives it some authority, but the investigator has no idea ahead of time what the person will say.

6. Investigators tend to take less thorough notes when there is an audio recording and may spend inordinate amounts of expensive time reviewing the audio to write up their report.

7. If there is litigation, the recording may be admissible as a business record, when normally the person's out-of-court statement would be inadmissible hearsay.

8. Recordings open the organization to criticism of the quality of the investigation.

9. Recordings are difficult and expensive to transcribe. While there are businesses that provide automated transcripts, there may be confidentiality concerns. And when a court reporter is not present at the time to ask for clarifications, spellings, or repetitions, the work quality is affected.

As you are thinking through the decision, counsel can help you analyze what would work best. You may choose to have a policy or evaluate on a case-by case basis. In any case, it is best that recordings not be shared with witnesses (similar to all the other investigative documents). If they want their own recording, they can also do that.

Do You Need Permission to Record?

Whether you can record without consent depends on the law in the jurisdiction. It is best to record openly and obtain consent to avoid potential problems. There are some exceptions, but these should be discussed with legal counsel. Best practices are:

1. Ask permission initially.
2. Keep the recorder in view.
3. With the recorder running, state the date, time, and place of the interview, and the name of the interviewer and witness.
4. Get consent from the witness on the recording.
5. At the end of the interview, you may want to have the witness confirm that the interview was recorded with consent.

All documents related to the investigation should be stored in a highly confidential place and kept in accordance with the document storage policy.

CHAPTER 9

Wrapping Up the Investigation

Should the Investigation Generate a Final Written Report?

Most of the time, a written report is a good idea for the organization's records. In some situations, a written report might not be necessary, for example, in a minor matter. But if there is a chance that the issue could lead to liability for the organization, having a written report reinforces that it did its due diligence in the investigation. A report provides documentation for the ultimate decision and outcome of the investigation.

There are pitfalls in written reports. An investigator may make the following mistakes:

1. Fail to make factual findings and write everything down without evaluating credibility. This leaves the reader to sift through the evidence and draw conclusions.

2. Write up findings in a way that is unnecessarily damaging to the organization or fails to support a thorough investigation.
3. Reach legal conclusions (particularly undesirable if the investigator is not a lawyer).
4. Make findings that are contrary to the existing evidence.

Finalizing the Investigation and Drafting Reports

After the investigator has gathered all the information, he or she will use the information to make findings and decide what is more likely than not to have happened. Information and findings are typically captured in a set of documents.

Investigators will create an investigative file, containing the materials reviewed. There will be a memo or summary of each interview. These should be factual, contain relevant direct quotes, and avoid inflammatory language. They will contain a credibility evaluation but otherwise avoid expressing opinions. Summaries can also note the demeanor and body language of the witness, where relevant. Investigators can record significant events, like crying, shouting, refusal to answer questions, evasiveness, and so on. Once the memo/summary of each interview is finished, the underlying notes will likely not be kept (but rely on advice of counsel regarding work product).

The interview memos are generally used to generate a Statement of Findings or Master Report. This will be a detailed (and maybe quite lengthy) factual analysis of different allegations, perhaps divided into relevant sections. The document will note how complaints were made and provide a chronology of events. It will summarize the identities of people involved, nature of the complaints, any pertinent background, a summary of organizational policies, timelines, and other relevant information. The report will include details about the investigation, including dates, investigators involved, persons present at interviews, and so on. It will include credibility determinations, and perhaps a credibility matrix. Also included will be a list of documents relied upon and witnesses interviewed.

The report will determine what is substantiated and what cannot be corroborated and note factual conclusions. It may also note issues that could not be resolved. It will evaluate whether policies and internal controls were followed, and any early organizational response.

Normally, legal conclusions and recommendations will not included, especially by non-attorney investigators. Recommendations can be made verbally to legal counsel. Factual findings should use words like *inappropriate, unprofessional*, or *policy violation*, as opposed to *harassment, discrimination, negligence, wrongdoing*, or other legally significant terms.

The report should be reviewed by counsel and HR professionals before finalizing. To be clear, this is not for the purpose of changing evidence gathered or factual findings made. Sometimes there is additional important information that investigators have not become aware of. Other times, conclusions may not be supportable as a matter of fact and law—or they are supportable, but the Report does not explain clearly enough how conclusions were made. Therefore, some discussion and revision can be beneficial to improve the work product.

Considering Legal Conclusions

If an attorney is involved, he or she can create a separate legal memorandum, marked attorney-client privileged and confidential work product. This memo can include the attorney's mental impressions and legal conclusions. It can make recommendations for discipline or policy recommendations for the organization. It can analyze potential legal liability. Another approach may be for an attorney to give a verbal debriefing to in-house counsel or to HR.

Information about the Investigation to Participants

What information should be given to those who participated in the investigation? While not required, it is fairly common and may be helpful to provide findings in some form to the reporting person (and person harmed, if different) and the person accused. These findings can be a brief Statement of Findings of what was found as it relates to them personally. Those writing up these communications must be cautious to protect the privacy of other persons as appropriate and legally required.

The reporting person's brief findings can cover whether the complaint was verified and whether action was taken. Whether the reporting person receives details may depend on the nature of the complaint, whether he or she continues to work with the alleged offender, and so on. Generally, the reporting person doesn't have the right to know whether and how other employees were disciplined, but does have the right to be assured that a safety plan is in place.

Normally, other witnesses are not provided with any written documents, as it is typically best practice not to discuss personnel matters with those outside the "need to know" circle.

A person accused may also be informed whether allegations were substantiated, perhaps in a brief Statement of Findings.

Information about Offenders

In missions or other ministry work, a related question often arises about what to tell the sending church, supporters, or church members, particularly if the allegations are substantiated. Each case should be dealt with individually and with the advice of legal counsel. Publicizing misconduct too widely can lead to legal liability in the form of defamation and other similar claims from the person accused. Plus, even in a good investigation, unless there is rock-solid evidence (such as a confession), there is always a chance that findings can be misinterpreted or are mistaken.

On the other hand, there is great concern about "passing the trash" in the case of serious allegations like child abuse. There is at least a moral obligation (though rarely a legal one) to provide warning about predators to other organizations.[1] It may be important to have careful communications with other organizations about findings and possible risks.

Duties of the Point Person

An organizational point person also has responsibilities in closing out an investigation. Reporting persons should be informed that the investigation has been resolved. The organization may need to engage in disciplinary follow-up. Persons accused and victims should be informed of the results as it pertains to them. If harm was not substantiated, persons bringing those allegations should be informed of the finding. There still may be a safety plan or assistance in resolving trauma.

Dealing with Unsubstantiated Claims in the Workplace

Seeking the truth can be difficult and complex, and the investigation may or may not turn out as the reporting witness hoped.

At the conclusion of an investigation, the "finding" will be that certain actions happened either by a preponderance of the evidence, which means that it more likely than not happened, or by clear and convincing evidence, which is a higher standard. If the standard hasn't been met, the organization won't take disciplinary action against the person. It is possible that you may be pretty sure that abuse did not happen. It's also possible that the whole situation is too murky to be sure of the facts. Especially with things that happened long ago and far away, you may have to accept that you will never know. Supposing that the impartial workplace investigation suggests that Ms. Complaining Witness is actually herself the problem. One possibility is that she was malicious. If Ms. Complaining Witness has fabricated accusations against people, she can be disciplined. If Ms. Complaining Witness is engaging in deliberate or accidental problematic behavior, she can be counseled, put on a performance plan, or receive other actions that HR believes is appropriate for administering the level of discipline required.

Ms. Complaining Witness may have formed an opinion about someone else that turned out to be incorrect, because she was mistaken or did not have all the facts. She can be told that a careful investigation was done, but other information has become available showing that her suspicions were not substantiated (probably drafted with the help of your counsel). However, in this case, Ms. Complaining Witness would not be disciplined.

Documentation must be very careful and thorough, and this must be approached wisely, to avoid a claim of retaliation.

How do we follow up with unsubstantiated claims? Let's split the response into two areas: the impact on the career and life of the accused and the impact on the reporting person.

It is morally wrong to ruin someone's life and career because of an allegation that is not substantiated. (In some circumstances, it could also be illegal.) You will have the delicate task of preserving the person's career and reputation, even though you might not be completely sure that the allegation is untrue. And of course, if a safety plan is necessary, that could also have some impact on the person's career that you cannot help, such as when they are not allowed to work with children. In addition, the investigation will be preserved in the files, in case you get more evidence or further allegations later. How you handle the situation depends partly on your safety plan and partly on whether the matter is really uncertain or it's pretty certain that the person is innocent.

There is also an impact on the person making the allegation, whose allegation has not been substantiated. It is fairly common that allegations cannot be substantiated. The allegation may have a basis of truth but because of time and distance cannot be substantiated. Sometimes memories of actual events have become intensified to where actions are perceived as abusive, when at the time they were more likely seen as unwise or inappropriate. Or actions may have happened that would not have been considered abuse in the historical framework but would be considered abusive in our time. Or the person bringing the complaint is not interpreting events as a reasonable person would. Or there can be memory or credibility issues. Allegations that are deliberately untrue are relatively rare.

In any of these scenarios, the person bringing the accusation is hurting, and reporting back to the person should be handled with great sensitivity. In addition, the person may need help and support (therapy or pastoral care). It may also be necessary to make some changes in the work environment, if people are not going to be able to work together.

Dealing with Unsubstantiated Child Abuse Claims

Suppose an adult or a teen at a church is accused of molesting a child, and the authorities drop the case without taking any action. Social services and law enforcement agencies typically will not share any information with the church about what they did or did not find. But the parents of the child may still insist that the alleged offender be barred from the church. In some cases, certain individuals will go on a campaign to ruin the reputation of someone they believe is an offender.

How is the organization to determine if there has really been abuse? Sometimes it is necessary for the organization to have its own independent investigation. This may or may not create certainty.

Sometimes it is not even possible to conduct an independent investigation. For instance, parents might or might not allow you to talk to a child, but you will be unable to get a meaningful interview if the parents have been discussing the alleged abuse with the child for weeks.

(This could also be why the authorities did not pursue the matter.) Or if the person bringing allegations has serious mental health issues or recovered memory, it may not be possible to interview the person, or an interview may not produce useful results.

Another possible approach is to have a psychological evaluation of persons involved, if they consent. Someone who is accused of being an offender can undergo a sex offender evaluation. This can determine whether they have deviant sexual interests and/or whether they are a current danger to children. Someone who may be a victim can undergo an evaluation for trauma. Evaluations such as these are done by people with forensic expertise in evaluating sex offenders or in evaluating children for trauma. While such evaluations are expensive, they can help to provide assurance that the organization is taking reasonable approaches on safety.

A similar approach is to have a person accused voluntarily take a polygraph or lie detector test. While not admissible in court, they can provide useful evidence in a disciplinary situation. But keep in mind that there is a reason that polygraphs are not admissible in evidence; they are not always reliable.

In a ministry setting where the person accused is a minister, the organization is going to have more leverage to require participation in these unusual approaches. Requiring consent would be tricky in a typical workplace setting.

If a claim is unsubstantiated, it is not appropriate to discipline someone accused. But you will still ask: If the investigation is inconclusive or has concluded nothing happened, is there still a risk of harm to children? If you thought there was a small chance that abuse happened—say, 20 or 30 percent—you would still want to put in place a safety plan. Even if nothing can be determined in the investigation, you would not take a chance on child safety (see chapter 4 for more information). For example, the organization may choose not to allow the person to work with children going forward, while still allowing other types of professional or volunteer work. Or if there has been a sexual harassment allegation, it may be wise to keep persons separated. This type of safety plan requires careful analysis so that people are not treated unjustly.

If a claim is unsubstantiated, the organization may need to deal with issues of gossip or "campaigns" to destroy someone who is accused. If the allegations cannot be substantiated and the person will not stop lobbying against the accused, there may need to be church discipline.

CHAPTER 10

LEADERSHIP RESPONSIBILITIES, RESTORATION, AND RECONCILIATION

A Communication Dilemma

The board of Church Christian School (CCS) engaged in a sobering meeting after having received an investigative report. CCS had been in existence for 30 years. They just found out that for 10 of those years, a pedophile teacher had sexually abused girls going through the third and fourth grades. As many as 50 children might have been abused. The perpetrator was dead, so not much could happen from that perspective. The headmaster at the time of the abuse had since retired.

The board considered the following actions: issue a public report that would let alumni and parents know what had happened; offer individual apologies to the survivors who had come forward; hold a survivors' retreat; and establish a counseling fund. Should the previous headmaster separately write an apology for missing this abuse? Would these actions bring healing or make matters worse?

Leadership Responsibilities

The board (or comparable leadership) has important fiduciary duties as well as spiritual responsibilities. It will develop a plan based on the factual findings. The plan will outline how to discipline wrongdoers, minister to victims and those close to them, protect others at risk, vindicate anyone exonerated, extend compassion to those who may not be victims, protect confidentiality, and avoid liability for the organization.

One reason investigators should not be given the power to make recommendations or insist on particular discipline is that it abrogates the responsibility of leadership, which in the case of a ministry is also a spiritual authority. It is often helpful to consult legal counsel in making these decisions, but legal counsel should also support the spiritual authority of leadership and consider the spiritual goals of the organization.

Here are some possible response steps that could be taken in response to an investigation:

1. Training for organizational personnel.
2. Paid leave for staff harmed.
3. Counseling services for survivor and survivor's family.
4. Pastoral counseling for survivors or others harmed.
5. Revision of policies.
6. Training for staff, volunteers, and even children.
7. Change of management.
8. Some form of Christian conciliation.
9. A restorative justice retreat.

10. Written disciplinary letter for offender or those who created an unsafe environment.
11. Coaching for offender.
12. Termination of offender.

Those who have offended should be disciplined, possibly terminated, depending on the level of the offense. Minor offenses may call for training or apologies. This also applies to leaders who have failed to keep people safe, depending on the level of culpability involved.

Care for those harmed is more important even than disciplining the offender. People often need counseling, pastoral outreach, and expressions of care from the congregation. Care for those harmed is a long-term process. It doesn't involve just a couple of meetings. Abuse creates long-term trauma, and for serious situations, the organization will need to be invested in the response over time.

Consider working with people trained in responding to victims, specifically experts experienced in providing research-based trauma care. This is an important new field in psychology. Again, if you don't have internal experts, reach out to find trained professionals. Being insensitive toward those who have been harmed can make the trauma worse.

Restoration and Discipline for the Offender

Ministries often wonder if there should be restoration for an offender. The answer is both yes and no. Is there forgiveness in Christ for the repentant? Absolutely, and Christians have a duty to forgive those who repent, just as the Lord has forgiven all who are sincerely contrite. Does this mean going back to the status quo? Usually not, where allegations are serious and substantiated.

Think of a recovering alcoholic. If a man has been two years sober after having suffered for years from active alcoholism, it would not be wise to encourage him to work in a bar or a liquor store. Likewise, offenders of any kind should not be exposed to temptation.

Both the ministry and the offender must do hard work. Facing up to the damage that sin has done often means engaging in a long, slow process of making changes and seeking healing. Taking care of victims often means a safety plan and healing plan for them. The safety of those harmed is more important than reinstating the offender, because even seeing the offender can cause further trauma for the harmed individual. Protecting others often means not giving further access to an offender. The board must also realistically confront personality disorders, addictive disorders, and other deep-rooted issues.

Restoration is often costly, financially and relationally. One can define restoration in three ways. The first pertains to *relationship*. Restoration is not possible in relationship if one person is not repentant or another person is not willing or able to forgive. In one situation, a now-adult victim went back and confronted the man who had seduced and sexually abused him as a teenager. The man acknowledged his actions but refused to admit that there was anything wrong with his behavior. Although the victim was willing to forgive if a sincere request for forgiveness had been asked for, no restoration was possible because of lack of repentance.

In other cases, victims are not able to work through the difficult process of forgiveness or simply are not willing to. It's important to add the caveat that even if there has been some restoration in the relationship, full restoration may not be possible. If the relationship has not been healthy, it would not be wise to have the same depth in the relationship or the same access to the person. There may even be legal liability for allowing an abusive person access to a survivor.

The second aspect of restoration involves *position*. This means returning an individual to the previously held position within the organization, which may not be appropriate. If a person has committed a serious offense, he may not be eligible for positional restoration into leadership, either for a period of time or forever. This does not speak to God's forgiveness, but to our practical realities. It also speaks to who is allowed to be a role model to others. Wrongly rushing into positional restoration can create extensive harm to people already traumatized, as well as legal liability if the person offends again. For instance, the standard is zero tolerance for child sexual abuse. An adult who has sexually abused children is safest never to be in interpersonal ministry again, whether or not he has a genuine repentance.

From a scriptural perspective, the Bible presents very specific requirements for a leader, many of which can be found in the third chapter of 1 Timothy. From a legal perspective, an organization can be responsible for negligent supervision if it gives an abuser or someone guilty of other destructive behaviors an opportunity for further wrongdoing.

The third definition of restoration involves *location*. It may not be possible or wise to restore a person to a particular location. For instance, if the person's behavior has been triggered by stressors in that location, that place is likely not right for them. Or suppose there is an allegation of abuse but the allegation is found inconclusive. If you believe there is a 30 percent chance that the person has abused a child, you might not terminate the person but would likely remove the person from locations where he or she had access to children. This would not be a disciplinary action but a safety plan action. One approach may be to have a forensic psychological evaluation done of an alleged offender to obtain guidance on risk factors. When allegations are not substantiated, if there is a choice between who should suffer, an adult or a child, or a leader versus a member, a spiritually mature leader will be willing to suffer to protect the innocent.

True repentance by an offender requires the willingness to work through these steps despite the pain and patience required. An attitude of offering a quick apology and getting back to ministry is not true repentance. Someone who has harmed others needs to go through the process of realizing the depth of that harm and the slow healing involved.

Sometimes we hear the phrase "under the blood" used as an excuse to ignore abusive behavior, because it has been forgiven. It is true that our sins are forgiven under Christ's blood. That does not change the hard work of facing up to the damage sin has done, taking care of victims, putting in place safety plans, working through one's personality disorders, and generally doing the hard work of restoration. Christ's blood was costly and so is restoration on the human level. And we must remember that spiritual restoration does not mean that the person can always stay in his job.

Sharing the Investigation with the Public

The Master Report should be carefully considered by leadership and by the board, with a view toward improving the organization, correcting past mistakes, and seeking healing. But there may be pressure for an organization to share the Master Report with the public, and some people believe this should always happen. This position appears to be based on the premise that the organization should be publicly accountable.

Normally, it is not advisable to disseminate the full, detailed written report to participants in the investigation, let alone post it online. Sharing too much publicly presents many serious concerns. Even though the names of those harmed or abused are rarely shared, the level of detail in a Master Report often raises prurient interest, and people can and do figure out who the survivors are and what happened to them. In addition, sharing details about an employee from a personnel investigation is legally risky. Master Reports often include allegations and criticisms going in all directions, including about complainants or other witnesses.

Providing the Master Report widely likely waives any privilege in the investigation, which may also create legal risk for the organization.

Given that an investigation is only done to preponderance of the evidence, there are potentially justice issues in sharing the names of those determined to be offenders—especially if the evidence is not extremely strong. Even if allegations have been substantiated, because of the lower standard of preponderance, there is still a good possibility they may not be true. And there is substantial risk of a defamation lawsuit for making untrue statements about an offender (see Appendix A). The organization may get called upon to defend the truth of its statements, calling the investigation into question. Great consideration needs to be given to whether naming offenders publicly is wise.

Privacy issues are relevant for both survivors and alleged offenders. What can be shared is different when there are only allegations versus findings. It also makes a difference what is in the public record, such as a criminal conviction, or how solid the findings are. Barely making a "more likely than not" standard may elicit a different response than having "clear and convincing" evidence.

In cases where there is a broad group of stakeholders, such that some public accountability is wise, a Summary Report can be produced. Such a report can discuss the overall investigation, findings, and culture of the organization without revealing personal details. This is as much information as the general public is entitled to.

Who needs to know what happened? And how much do they need to know? Perhaps the congregation needs to know something. Perhaps certain leaders within the congregation need to know more. Other possible victims may need enough information to encourage them to come forward. Other children or other victims must be kept safe.

Lessons Learned

At the end of an investigation, it is a good idea to review organizational policies and procedures to see where improvements can be made. Cultural issues, policies, or systems can all be evaluated for change.

In addition, it is helpful to have an After-Action Report or evaluation of the investigation itself. No investigations are perfect and there are always new things to be learned.

Reconciliation

Often, after an investigation, there is a desire to encourage reconciliation between the persons involved. Many factors play into this: whether persons involved will still be working together, how serious the behavior was, how badly traumatized the person was, and so on.

Religious organizations do have some leeway here to follow scriptural standards for reconciliation but should be wary of placing too many requirements on the reporting person or the person harmed. From a legal perspective, sometimes even a request that the reporting person attend some sort of session with the accused can later look like retaliation in a lawsuit. Make sure these things are voluntary and not job dependent.

Organizational Apologies

Apologies can be an important aspect of restoration. They may lead to forgiveness but not always. An apology must consider what people are looking for.

1. Has the underlying problem been fixed? For example, have child safety policies and training been put in place?
2. Have people been appropriately disciplined?
3. Is the organization willing to repair harm by taking restorative action?

If the organization is going to apologize, it must do so authentically. This requires acknowledging the offense, apologizing unconditionally, not minimizing the harm, expressing genuine remorse, and taking responsibility. If no one is currently at the organization who is responsible for the harm, the organization will need to practice "identification repentance," personally accepting responsibility for what the organization did in the past.

Offering a survivor the opportunity to meet with a high-level leader and personally receive an apology can be helpful. (For more information about apologies, see the "Restoring Shalom" talk in Telios Teaches, accessible through the QR code provided on the Telios Teaches page at the back of this book.)

Other Forms of Healing

Once the investigation is over, the organization should consider healing measures. An employer may consider offering other support to the reporting party, like counseling or time off, no matter what the outcome. This can help demonstrate the organization's goodwill and commitment to member care.

Christian mediation can be helpful if all parties are willing to engage in it. A trained Christian mediator can help bring reconciliation and healing. However, caution must be used not to pressure people to participate.

In abuse situations or difficult work situations, the organization may want to fund counseling or support services for survivors. This should be carefully structured to allow the survivor to choose the counselor but to make sure that the professional has adequate credentials.

Some organizations have provided for a professionally hosted retreat for restorative justice and healing. This can be helpful if there is a group of survivors, such as a group of missionary kids. However, it must be structured carefully so that survivors feel safe and are not retraumatized. In cases of widespread abuse, some kind of memorial might be appropriate.

CONCLUSION

I f you have formed the impression that responding to allegations is complicated, time-consuming, expensive, or easy to get wrong, you are correct. An investigation, for example, requires considerable effort. But it can also bring justice for victims, hold offenders accountable, and offer the kind of closure that only the truth can. A well-done investigation can equip an organization with the tools to move forward redemptively.

It's easy to see allegations and the response process as a distraction from the ministry of the church or other religious organization. Time and resources get diverted from the "real" goal of the spreading the gospel and thus seem to be wasted. But consider this: Addressing sin, helping the vulnerable, bringing healing—are these not part of building the Kingdom of God? In any endeavor, some of the most backbreaking work is destructive—weeding or pruning in the garden or dismantling the bathroom wall to uncover mold or plumbing mistakes. But it is a necessary prelude to the constructive work of healing and rebuilding. Finding truth and setting people free is also the work of Christ, as well as preaching the gospel. God calls us to participate in his mission of righteousness:

> to open the eyes that are blind,
> to bring out the prisoners from the dungeon,
> from the prison those who sit in darkness.[1]

APPENDIX A

ALLEGED OFFENDERS STRIKE BACK: AVOIDING DEFAMATION CLAIMS

In the sexual assault or child sexual abuse arena, the alleged victim sues an organization for claims such as negligent supervision. But there can also be lawsuits by the alleged offenders.

For example, a student athlete at Xavier University filed a lawsuit alleging that a female student falsely accused him of sexual assault.[1] No one denied there was a sexual encounter, but he says that it was completely consensual. The university, which was under scrutiny from the Office for Civil Rights, expelled the student and made a public announcement that the student was "responsible for a serious violation of the Code of Student Conduct."

The former student said that the university failed to follow its own policies, conducted an unfair hearing, and defamed him by what it published. In denying the university's motion to dismiss, the court based its decision partly on the fact that the county prosecutor had investigated and found no evidence of sexual assault, and partly on potential due process problems with the hearing. (The result has come under extensive criticism for not being sufficiently pro-victim.)

Organizations should not assume that accusations are necessarily true. More often than not, they are, but not always. They can be untrue for many reasons, from spite to incorrect memories to attention-seeking. Investigations must be objective and impartial.

Defamation requires a "false" statement. Internal investigations evaluate whether the alleged misconduct "more likely than not" happened. These findings are not made in a court of law. And they may

be relatively easy to challenge, because any flaws in the investigation may move the findings from over 50 percent likelihood to under 50 percent likelihood. The defamation lawsuit will end up being mainly about the truth or falsity of the statements.

Organizations should be sure that their investigations offer due process to the accused. The person accused should have the chance to present his side, including evidence and witnesses. Even though it is not a criminal trial, a finding of sexual misconduct can ruin a person's life and career.

Organizations must be very careful about public statements, as even a statement relatively lacking in detail can be challenged. Whether to make any statement at all should be carefully evaluated with counsel.

Religious organizations have more freedom than secular organizations to follow their religious internal judicial process without having the courts second-guess their decisions. The more formal the process and the more rooted in religious principles, the less likely that secular courts will wish to be entangled with the ecclesiastical court or appeal. Canonical trials, for instance, are very structured and highly protected by clergy confidentiality. As such, they are a model for effective and confidential internal proceedings.

APPENDIX B

CHILD SEXUAL ABUSE AND BIBLICAL ETHICS

Roger L. Dixon, M.Div., Th.M., Ph.D.
Theresa Lynn Sidebotham, J.D.

Introduction

This section addresses biblical ethics when the crime of child abuse (particularly sexual abuse) occurs in a Christian church, mission, or school. In many countries, including the United States, the definition and parameters of child abuse are established in criminal law. When crimes occur across jurisdictions or happened a long time ago, they are often not addressed by government authorities. Under these circumstances, an internal investigation by the religious organization becomes necessary, because it is the only accountability for the harm. Biblical disciplinary decisions must be made under the ethics and policies of the mission or religious organization involved. A number of common questions arise about biblical ethics and the appropriateness of secular actions such as abuse reporting or employment investigations.

General Ethics Undergirding Investigation and Punishment of Child Sexual Abuse

Criminal codes define child abuse, and broad consensus exists nationally and internationally about definitions of child abuse, including child sexual abuse. Religious organizations accept or elaborate on these definitions and follow the criminal codes of their own jurisdictions. Child protection policies will have definitions of child abuse that are consistent with the responsibility of good citizens.

How should a religious organization ethically respond to allegations of child abuse? The Markkula Center for Applied Ethics, a leader in research and dialogue surrounding nonprofit ethics, lists four principles that help to provide a framework.[1]

1. Protect the victim and potential victims.
2. Do justice for the victim.
3. Bring the accused to justice.
4. Protect the organization.

A religious organization's first responsibility is to the alleged victim, and the first two principles reflect this. Once an allegation has been made, the alleged victim must be protected as if the allegation were true. The alleged offender must have no further access to children who may be at risk, until after an investigation either by law enforcement or within the organization, and then only if the investigation reveals that there is not a safety risk.

Justice must be done for the alleged victim. In some countries, justice is carried out by law enforcement or child protection services. In other jurisdictions, this may not be possible because of local law or because the crimes happened outside of jurisdiction. Enforcement may also be hindered in historical cases where the allegations are very old and the alleged victim is no longer a child. If government will not be involved, the organization will need to take action. Whether or not the investigation ends in a clear determination, justice can also be done for the alleged victim by providing counseling and support.

While the Markkula Center expresses the third principle as bringing the accused to justice, seeking justice for the accused is a more accurate way to express it. Religious organizations want justice for the accused whether the accused is guilty or innocent of the charge. If the former, then the accused will hopefully be brought to justice by the government, and if the latter, the accused should have an opportunity to show his innocence. Even if the government is not involved, the religious organization can make disciplinary decisions. The religious organization is also responsible for providing due process to the accused by giving the accused the opportunity to tell his story, present witnesses, and generally experience a fair procedure.

The fourth principle calls for protecting the organization. This means several things. First, the organization must protect its mission and integrity, which means preserving its high ethical standards and commitment to the safety of children. Next, the organization should protect against reputational and legal harm, meaning that it should deal with the problems responsibly in a way that protects the organization's public image and shows that it is not negligent. A church or mission must have ethical standards for protecting the vulnerable in its care and should follow best practices and legal standards, which will also protect the organization. To have a strong Christian testimony, organizations must take allegations of child abuse seriously and act upon them.

Ethics and a Biblical Worldview about Children

Being concerned about child abuse flows from the nature of God. God defends the vulnerable.[2] God loves justice, and wicked acts have consequences.[3] God provides the civil authorities to rule an orderly society, and believers are to be subject to the civil authorities. The authorities swing the sword as God's servants, bringing terror to wrongdoers.[4]

God highly values children. Jesus welcomed little children.[5] He had harsh words for anyone who would cause a child to stumble: "But whoever causes one of these little ones who believe in me to sin, it would be better for him to have a great millstone fastened around his neck and to be drowned in the depth of the sea."[6] As Senior Pastor Ron Hawkins stated, "If the church does not address these issues by giving biblical instruction, warning, and direction, it ignores aspects of the teaching of the Word of God and a great area of need in the culture."[7]

While in times past, not much was known or understood about child sexual abuse, cultural and organizational knowledge have developed greatly in the last 15-20 years. If religious organizations knowingly fail to care for and protect children, they share to some degree the guilt of offenses against children. The principles that Jesus taught about children are based on the word of God from ancient times. For instance, in Ezekiel, God condemned the actions of Jerusalem in injuring God's own children by participating in pagan child sacrifice: "And you took your sons and your daughters, whom you had borne to me, and these you sacrificed to them to be devoured. Were your whorings so small a matter that you slaughtered my children and delivered them up as an offering by fire to them?"[8] Children belong to God, and their protection is so important that an adult should not be protected from punishment if he or she is guilty of child sexual abuse.

Internal and Governmental Approaches in Handling Allegations of Abuse

Religious organizations generally have two avenues for handling allegations of child abuse: governmental and internal. Both are scripturally appropriate, as their common purpose is to expose the guilty and establish justice. Religious organizations have always had to confront evil. The writer Jude pointed this out when he noted, "For certain people have crept in unnoticed who long ago were designated for this condemnation, ungodly people, who pervert the grace of our God into sensuality and deny our only Master and Lord, Jesus Christ."[9]

Engaging with governmental authorities in response to allegations of child abuse often begins by reporting the suspected abuse to civil authorities. Sometimes religious organizations do not report abuse, believing that problems should be handled internally. Although problems should also be handled internally, as sin produces consequences within the church, Christians are told to obey the civil authorities because God has established them.[10] Reporting crimes to the governmental authorities complies with the law in the many cases where reporting is mandatory. Even if reporting is not required, reporting crimes allows the governmental authority to exercise its scriptural role in punishing bad conduct and creating a safe environment.

Engaging in an internal investigation also complies with legal and scriptural principles. On the legal side, employers have both the right and the duty to carry out internal investigations to have a healthy and legally compliant workplace. If they do not uphold this responsibility, they may rightly be held accountable in a civil lawsuit.

On the scriptural side, religious organizations also have the responsibility and authority to carry out internal discipline, protecting the vulnerable and holding members accountable to religious standards. Scripture gives the church the right to judge and settle disputes internally, and specifically to pronounce judgment on sexual immorality (such as child sexual abuse).[11] Thus, an organization should either use information from the government's investigation or carry out its own inquiry in order to make a sound judgment. Yet we must understand that the investigations are different in nature—we are not investigating crimes, and the government is not making decisions about internal misconduct.

Questions of Grace and Forgiveness

Churches and missions sometimes bring up the idea of dispensing grace when allegations of abuse surface. Religious organizations have frequently fallen into the trap of giving sexual predators a second chance to be in ministry around children because the perpetrator has "repented." In the past, churches often approached child sexual abuse in this way, and the consequences were devastating. Even so, some churches still argue for this approach today.

But Christians are required to be wise in handling the wolves that attack the sheep, which is a perfect description of someone who commits child sexual abuse.[12] In particular, research shows that it is difficult to be certain that those who commit child sexual abuse will not repeat the offense, as "sexual offenders are at risk of reoffending for a long period of time."[13] High-level professional intervention does make a difference in recidivism.[14]

Still, while there may be grace in the sense of assuring a repentant person that he is forgiven, there cannot be grace in allowing him or her access to children again. The only way to keep children safe is to have zero tolerance for child sexual abuse. Repentant alcoholics should not be allowed to tend the bar, and child sexual abusers should not have access to children. Regardless of the actual risk of recidivism, once that trust has been broken, the legal risk to the organization in allowing a sex offender access to children would be enormous.

To be clear, this does not necessarily mean barring a sexual offender from church. Some churches are able to commit to discipleship programs for sex offenders that include high-level professional treatment and monitoring. Some treatment programs are effective and can include regular polygraph maintenance, which is an option that church organization should consider if they are willing to integrate the sex offender back into their congregation. In addition, the prognosis for successful reintegration is going to be better for an offender who is willing to be open with the entire church about his offense. Admitting the offense helps keep children safe and also shows genuine repentance.

Sometimes the question is raised of what to do when the sexual abuse is not fully established. In an internal employment investigation (like a civil lawsuit), the standard of evidence is usually preponderance of the evidence, or more likely than not. Some argue that this standard is unjust. A person's career may be ended because of a slightly more than 50 percent probability that he committed child sexual abuse.

In cases like this, where there is a potential for injustice to one or the other, the religious organization must choose whether to protect the adult or the children. A moment's reflection shows that those who care for children will not want them exposed to someone for whom there is a 55 percent probability (or perhaps even a 30 percent probability) that he or she has sexually abused children. Where one must choose between protecting vulnerable children or the career of an adult, protecting the children must come first. This is true even if there are pre-existing loyalties to the adult.

Another aspect of this problem is that frequently the adult who is being accused—even if falsely—has engaged in behavior in violation of child safety policies or unwise behavior, creating the appearance of evil. Titus 1:6 requires that elders be above reproach. Someone may not have met this standard, even if it is not fully established that they have sexually abused a child.

Godly leaders understand that a good shepherd lays down his life for the sheep.[15] If someone is falsely accused, God will vindicate him or her someday, but children cannot be put at risk.

Interpretation of Scriptures about Managing Conflict

In dealing with issues of child abuse, Christians must consider the direction of Scripture on aspects of conflict resolution and disciplining religious leaders, such as Matthew 18 and 1 Timothy 5. Matthew 18:15 describes an ecclesiastical process that requires the person offended to personally and directly confront a brother who has offended against the person as the first stage of conflict resolution. It is common, indeed almost routine, for those who have committed child sexual abuse to quote this as a mandatory biblical process by which child sexual abuse must be addressed within the Christian community.

Accepting this interpretation misunderstands the passage. Matthew 18 describes a process by which an individual privately confronts a brother who has sinned, for handling conflict in the church. Eric Barreto, professor of New Testament at Princeton Theological Seminary, describes it as a process of addressing and reconciling personal differences in love:

> In short, the steps Jesus lays out here are not a mere blueprint so much as a statement of communal values and an acknowledgment of both the frailty as well as the utter necessity of communal discernment. Love requires that we address the inevitable conflicts that will arise among us. It is not enough to sweep them under the rug and thus allow them to fester. Unaddressed conflicts can render a community unable to function as God hopes. But neither is rejection our first instinct. Separation is not to be taken lightly even when it proves necessary. [16]

So the context of this passage relates to reconciling miscellaneous personal differences.

Matthew 18 also describes a process between persons of equal status—in that day, men ("your brother")—who made decisions and judgments, served as witnesses, and so forth. It would not have been a culturally appropriate approach for persons of lesser power—in that day, woman, children, or slaves. Even today, approaching conflicts with love and communication discernment requires creating a safe approach for persons of little power, like children—which does not include a direct confrontation with persons of greater power.

Also, Matthew 18 does not address criminal activity or dangers to the public. Child abuse is not a personal conflict, but a serious crime that is "an urgent public concern."[17] Most churches would not consider Matthew 18 an appropriate process for handling robbery, rape, or murder. In each case, one could face criminal charges for covering up these crimes. Why would informal conflict resolution be considered appropriate for the crime of child sexual abuse? Child sexual abuse is a crime in all fifty states and most other countries—and failure to report it is also frequently a crime. As good citizens, we have an obligation to allow the authorities to do their job.

Matthew 18 goes on to warn against causing little ones to stumble and despising them, because their angels in heaven see the face of God.[18] To the contrary, it is appropriate for the leaders in the organization to step forth on behalf of the child, confront the individual, investigate the matter, and make a judgment that is spiritually sound and compliant with secular law.

Some religious organizations also misunderstand 1 Timothy 5:19, which says, "Do not admit a charge against an elder except on the evidence of two or three witnesses." And Deuteronomy 19:15, which requires at least two witnesses for conviction of a crime. Under this theory, those accused in religious organizations claim that they can never be disciplined for child sexual abuse (a crime that rarely happens in front of witnesses).

But even in Scripture, there are exceptions to this rule. The Mosaic Law has an example of a sexually abused young person trapped by a predator: "But if in the open country a man meets a young woman who is betrothed, and the man seizes her and lies with her, then only the man who lay with her shall die."[19] In this example, although there were no witnesses, the man could be disciplined for the rape. Similarly, the guilt of Achan in stealing holy or "devoted" treasure in the time of Joshua was established by casting lots, because there were no witnesses to his theft.[20] And the guilt of Amnon in raping his half-sister, Tamar, was assumed though there were no witnesses.[21]

Thus, religious leaders should not accept proof text arguments that crimes committed in secret cannot be subject to discipline by religious organizations if an investigation supports the allegation.

Use of Professionals in the Internal Investigation Process

When a church or mission organization responds to a complaint of child abuse, sometimes people complain when professionals are used, because this is "legal" and not "scriptural." Why would an organization use professionals such as attorneys, investigators, psychologists, and child forensic investigators?

First, the interpretation of doctrine lies with the religious leaders. Professionals are brought in not as a substitute for this expertise and spiritual authority, but instead, serve a different role, bringing in expertise that helps to reveal truth. Ultimately, this results in a better outcome.

How do these professionals work? In the context of the workplace, the internal employment investigation came about as a tool to sort through allegations about employees. Those investigating may be trained employees of the organization or outside professionals. And, following best practices, they bring particular skills to the investigative task. Since non-professionals do not have these skills, they often make significant mistakes based on their own understanding or expectations, which can cause serious harm to victims and put others at risk.

For example, for accuracy and reliability, interviewing a child usually requires someone with training in child forensic interviewing. Investigators must possess sufficient training to capture needed and valuable evidence from witnesses and to press with questions that will help evaluate credibility. For situations that involve alleged sexual offenders, a forensic psychologist with specialized expertise may be able to evaluate the alleged offender much more accurately than a lay person. Bias is another potential problem. Typically, organizations will involve an outside investigator, attorney, or both to avoid bias either in favor of the alleged victim or the accused. Religious leaders may seek outside counsel to advise them as they make spiritual decisions and disciplinary determinations so they can apply best practices, comply with legal standards, and protect the organization.

Using professionals to help reach the best decision is not an abdication of spiritual authority. All of these professionals are used to help the leaders of the organization make wise and godly decisions. Typically, these professionals are themselves believers and trained in scriptural approaches. But even if they are not, Christians use wise counsel in all sorts of endeavors, from medicine to education. It makes sense that organizations would use qualified and objective professionals to assist in these very difficult inquiries. The final decisions still rest with the spiritual leaders of the organization, but they will make better decisions when they receive the best possible information.

Conclusion

Biblical ethics are closely tied to general ethics when it comes to protecting children and punishing predators. Religious organizations ought to obey secular authorities regarding public duties, such as reporting crimes, while also conducting internal religious discipline through their own procedures. Both the public and internal responses to child sexual abuse must be handled well to ensure the safety of the children and keep the organization above reproach.

APPENDIX C

ATTORNEY-CLIENT PRIVILEGE AND WORK PRODUCT

What Is Attorney-Client Privilege?

Attorney-client privilege was developed so that people could talk openly with their lawyers and get legal advice. Society protects the attorney-client privilege to "encourage full and frank communication between attorneys and their clients and thereby promote broader public interests in the observance of law and administration of justice."[1]

Attorney-client privilege allows a client to keep certain communications absolutely confidential and refuse to disclose them to a third party. The attorney-client "privilege exists to protect not only the giving of professional advice to those who can act on it, but also the giving of information to the lawyer to enable him to give sound and informed advice."[2] Some courts limit privilege to communications directed toward a legal opinion, legal services, or assistance with some kind of legal proceeding.[3] Other courts also allow communications about business matters if they include an implied request for legal advice.[4]

Communications could be verbal, written, or electronic, and even tangible objects.[5] Any of these can be protected as long as they are communications that are made to facilitate the client's receiving professional legal services or assistance. They must also be made in confidence and not shared with other people.[6]

The privilege obviously includes communications between the client and the lawyer. Attorney-client privilege "protects not only the advice of the attorney to the client, but also the information communicated by the client that provides a basis for giving advice."[7]

A communication cannot be intended to be confidential if it is made through a medium that subjects it to disclosure to third parties. The classic example is personal communications sent on work email when there is a policy that work email is not confidential.[8] Another example would be talking about sensitive matters in a crowded restaurant or on a bus.

For example, if a mission's administrator communicates with an attorney about how to analyze a child sexual abuse investigation and what steps the mission should take, both sides of the conversation are privileged. What the administrator communicates is privileged because the lawyer needs that information to give sound legal advice, and the lawyer's advice is also privileged. But if the administrator broadly communicates what is going on to people who do not have a need to know, or sends out a needlessly detailed Statement of Findings, she will waive the privilege.

Who Is a "Lawyer" for the Privilege in the U.S. and Abroad?

In some jurisdictions, such as Texas, the definition of a lawyer is very broad—any person authorized to practice law, or "reasonably believed by the client to be authorized" to practice law, in any state or nation.[9] In other jurisdictions, it might only include an attorney licensed in that jurisdiction.

Generally, an attorney on the board should not give legal counsel in a misconduct situation, but of course can give good advice as a board member. Separating the roles of board member and counsel, without losing professional liability coverage, is tricky.

Under a broad definition, consultations with national lawyers in other countries would be privileged in your own country, but not under a narrow definition. In one case, the court granted privilege where the attorney was effectively French "in-house counsel," even though there was no clear French equivalent in the legal system, and where France did not recognize a privilege. (France makes a sharp distinction between in-house and outside counsel.) The court found there was still a functional equivalence and privilege under U.S. law.[10] But another court found that French in-house counsel communications were not privileged.[11]

A number of other countries do not recognize attorney-client privilege at all or may have a more limited form of the privilege, so local counsel must also provide assurances of privilege or confidentiality from their end.[12]

Often, the privilege includes agents or representatives of the lawyer who are not attorneys at all. For instance, typically an investigator proceeding at the direction of an attorney would be the agent of that attorney, and her communications would be privileged.[13] Usually, an agent of a lawyer would include not only the lawyer's staff, but others employed by the lawyer, such as co-counsel, outside consultants, or investigators. In most jurisdictions, the privilege extends to certain third parties who are necessary to giving legal advice, such as an accountant or a translator.

In an investigation for a mission, an outside consultant hired by a law firm, such as a media expert or private investigator, would probably be covered by the privilege. You may need a legal analysis to see what is privileged in your jurisdiction.

Are Communications with Our In-House Counsel Privileged?

Privileged communications with in-house counsel have always been a little tricky. Courts have a bias against finding privilege for in-house counsel. First, in-house counsel often advises on business as well as legal issues. Next, courts assume that companies will channel all their communications through in-house counsel to cloak documents unfairly with privilege when they are not really for legal advice.[14] To evaluate whether the communication is privileged, the general test for in-house counsel is "whether counsel was participating in the communications primarily for the purpose of rendering legal advice or assistance."[15]

In a European case, the court refused to apply the attorney-client privilege to communications between in-house counsel and employees, stating that an in-house attorney is less independent than outside counsel.[16] Another European case held just the opposite.[17] The risk of using in-house counsel is to do an investigation and later find it is not privileged.

When using in-house counsel, establish the privilege carefully. First, show the communication is about legal matters. Second, mark the communication clearly. Third, keep legal roles separate from business ones. If non-lawyers are undertaking activities at the instruction of in-house counsel, this instruction should be explicit. Finally, it is worth considering whether the investigation should be supervised by outside counsel, who reports back to inside counsel.

Who Can Talk to the Attorney within the Privilege?

The group within the privilege varies by jurisdiction. The common test used to be the "control group" test, in which only communications to the top-level employees or management of an organization, responsible for directing the company's actions, were privileged (which made it tough to do confidential investigations).[18] This test is still in place in a few jurisdictions, such as the state courts of Illinois.

More common now is the subject matter test, or some variation of it. Under the subject matter test, the employee's communication is considered to be that of the organization if first, "the employee makes the communication at the direction of his superiors in the corporation" and second, "where the subject matter upon which the attorney's advice is sought by the corporation and dealt with in the communication is the performance by the employee of the duties of his employment."[19]

What does this mean? The attorney, or those the attorney is directing, may talk to other employees or staff of the mission, and the conversations or written communications will still be privileged, as long as the purpose of the discussion is within the scope of the person's job.

For example, because child safety is the concern of all staff (which should be stated by policy), discussions with personnel about a child abuse investigation would fit in the "subject matter test."

Attorney-Client Privilege and Those Being Interviewed

In jurisdictions that use the subject matter test, the attorney-client privilege probably applies to interviews of employees. Note that the privilege belongs to the organization, not to the employee, which means the employee does not get to decide whether to later reveal conversation or documents about the privileged matter.[20] Only corporate officers or directors have the authority to waive the privilege.[21]

In order to keep these conversations privileged, counsel or their representatives should give what is called an *Upjohn* warning at the beginning of each interview. This means that when counsel, or individuals acting on counsel's behalf, interview employees, those persons should be warned that the privilege is in place, but that they are not being represented individually by the attorney and cannot claim or waive the privilege themselves.[22] This is important, because an employee who has acted improperly may believe that the attorney is his or her attorney, when in reality the attorney is only the organization's attorney. This raises all kinds of ethical and legal problems, up to and including separate lawsuits.

Another issue is the tension that telling employees they cannot talk about their interviews may violate labor laws, because that is part of the "conditions" of their employment. And from a trauma perspective, people may need a way to process the interview.

When persons are interviewed who are not part of the organization, there is usually no privilege. (Sometimes former employees may be included in the privilege. Conversations between an attorney and former employees may be covered, if the discussion relates to knowledge gained during the employment.)[23] This can be relevant when an organization is interviewing people who have since left. Because former employees are not in the same position as current employees, counsel will need to analyze to what extent the privilege applies, if at all.

When non-U.S. staff is interviewed, the law of their jurisdictions will have an impact. In some cases, the discussions may not be privileged, and in other cases, it will be privileged only for U.S. proceedings.

Despite the privilege, the underlying facts will be discoverable, but thoughts, methods, and legal advice will not be.

What Falls Outside Attorney-Client Privilege?

If communications do not facilitate professional legal services, they are generally not privileged, even if the attorney is included in the communication. For instance, emails where an attorney is merely copied, or policy discussion where the attorney is merely present, may not be privileged. If the subject of the email or the meeting has nothing to do with legal advice, and the attorney is simply one of the group, the communication will typically not be privileged.[24] (Conversely, at least in some jurisdictions, if the email does relate to a legal issue, it will likely be privileged even if the attorney is not copied on it.) Because investigations may have a wide geographic span and are done mostly in writing, identifying privileged communications is important.

What Happens If You Rely on the Investigation to Defend a Lawsuit?

Sometimes in an employment dispute—for instance, about sexual harassment—an organization will defend itself on the basis that it took reasonable care to prevent and promptly correct any harassing behavior. When an employer does this, it puts the thoroughness and competence of the investigation at issue, for a defense.

The employer cannot rely on the thoroughness of the investigation and at the same time shield discovery of the documents based on attorney-client privilege or work product protection.[25] If the attorney has been consulted about the investigation for legal advice but has not been deeply involved in the investigation, the attorney's communications (but not the investigation) will likely still be privileged. If the attorney has been personally directing and involved with the investigation, the privilege may be waived for all the work.

Some organizations have a separate investigating attorney who only gives the final report to the defense attorney. Then the defense attorney is the one who gives legal advice to the organization. Another approach is not to have an attorney involved in the investigation at all, but only in giving advice to the organization. The investigation will not be privileged, but the attorney's communications will be.

What Is "Work Product" Doctrine?

"Work product" is similar to attorney client privilege, but not identical. Long ago, someone had the clever idea of letting the attorney on the other side do all the interviews in an investigation so he didn't have to do it himself. Then he asked for all the statements and details of the investigation. The U.S. Supreme Court case that followed developed the "work product" doctrine, which is designed to protect an attorney's work for her client. It held that an attorney needs to assemble information, sift facts, prepare legal theories, and plan strategy without having to worry about revealing thoughts to the other side.[26] Work product is protected so that one side cannot get hold of (and take advantage of) the work of the other party's attorney.

As the doctrine has developed, core work product, which contains the attorney's mental impressions, opinions, and conclusions, is never produced to the other side. Other work product, which includes facts, may be produced under some circumstances, when the other party has "substantial need" for it and no way to get it easily.[27]

What Exactly Counts as "Work Product"?

"Work product" is "material prepared or mental impressions developed in anticipation of litigation or for trial."[28] The material is prepared by an attorney, or by someone else for the attorney, in anticipation of litigation.[29] Work product can also include communications made in anticipation of litigation or for trial.

How do you define whether it is in anticipation of litigation? The simple answer is that if "the document would not have been generated 'but for' litigation, it is privileged."[30] The complex answer is that courts spend a lot of time figuring this out and go different ways on the question.

Surprisingly, work product material need not come from the attorney herself. It can be developed by or for either the party or the party's attorney. The persons who may be involved can include attorneys, consultants, insurers, employees, or agents, among others.[31]

The notes, documents, and discussions of a child abuse investigation, for instance, would be work product as long as the investigation was done in anticipation of litigation and at the direction of an attorney.

Disputes may arise about whether material is work product. For instance, an investigation may be done in anticipation of litigation, but it may be argued that it is part of the regular course of business of the mission to investigate child abuse. Courts will vary on how they interpret this "dual-purpose" material.

Because of these potential disputes, work product should be clearly identified. An attorney's litigation file is rarely discoverable, so material gathered at the direction of the attorney and retained by the attorney is safer than keeping the same material in company files.[32] While an attorney's litigation file is probably the safest place to keep material, as far as discovery goes, the organization will only want to do this when litigation is fairly likely, because of the disadvantage of having incomplete files and documents stored in multiple locations.

Anticipating Litigation: Why Do We Have to Decide This?

Litigation must be reasonably anticipated to claim work product protection (but not attorney-client privilege).

To decide when litigation is reasonably anticipated, there are different tests. For instance, Texas provides a fairly common test with two factors. One, the circumstances must "indicate to a reasonable person that there is a substantial chance of litigation." Second, the person claiming work product protection must have "had a good faith belief that litigation would ensue."[33] With this good faith belief, a "party may reasonably anticipate suit being filed and prepare for the expected litigation before anyone manifests an intent to sue." There need not be actual notice or discussion of a lawsuit.

The work product privilege can apply even if litigation is not imminent, as long as "the primary motivating purpose behind the creation of the document was to aid in possible future litigation."[34] A "substantial chance of litigation" doesn't mean any particular statistical probability, but litigation must be more than an abstract possibility. A party could "reasonably anticipate suit being filed, and conduct an investigation to prepare for anticipated litigation, before a party manifests an intent to sue by filing suit."[35]

Privileging Investigative Team Communications

When a company conducts an internal investigation, if those conducting the investigation are acting at the direction of corporate supervisors to secure legal advice in anticipation of litigation, the material is probably privileged, under attorney-client privilege, work product, or both.[36] (The underlying facts will not be protected and will have to be disclosed.)

If the investigation has no purpose to seek legal advice, there will be no attorney/client privilege or work product. Also, if unnecessary third parties are in the interviews, any privilege may be waived.[37]

To have the privilege in place, the investigation should be structured for the purpose of seeking legal advice. The attorney should be fairly closely involved in supervising the investigation and gathering the findings in order to give legal advice to the organization. Employees who are on the investigative team or who are being interviewed should know that the information is being given for the purpose of getting legal advice.

Confidentiality agreements should be in place for the investigative team, if they are not part of the law firm. Determine who will do the interviewing, who will be interviewed, who will be present at the interview, and why their presence is necessary. Some interviews simply may not be privileged, which is helpful to know ahead of time.

Document Preservation and a Litigation Hold

If there is a reasonable anticipation of litigation, there must be a "litigation hold." Even if there is no litigation hold, most investigations should have a "document preservation" notice. You cannot do a good investigation if the documents have gone missing.

A litigation hold means that documents related to the matter may not be destroyed without possible sanctions from the court. This doctrine was developed to keep parties from "cleaning up the files" to destroy damaging evidence.

You cannot have it both ways. If you are claiming "work product" because litigation is anticipated, you cannot destroy documents. Your attorney will help you determine whether litigation is reasonably anticipated and work through placing a litigation hold if it is.

A litigation hold involves identifying documents in many forms (written and electronic) related to the subject matter of the litigation hold. These documents may not be shredded, and these emails may not be deleted.

If there is a litigation hold, documents from the investigation, such as report drafts and investigation notes, may not be destroyed. Care should be taken during the investigation as to what is created and what is said in the informal communications.

Discovery is expensive, so it helps if there is less material to produce. If litigation is anticipated, documents should be carefully organized and marked if privileged, which will help later when a privilege log must be created.

On the other hand, if litigation is not anticipated, the files can be cleaned up, but they will be fully producible in the event of litigation, unless they are privileged.

Counsel can help you work through whether you have work product protection, or need a litigation hold, based on your facts and the law in your jurisdiction. It helps to know this before the investigation.

Members on the Investigative Team from Another Organization

Outside team members, whether hired or volunteer, may be included in the privilege. A non-employee consultant's communication with mission employees may be included, if the consultant is acting for the mission and has the information needed by attorneys to give legal advice.[38] Each person's role should be defined carefully to show the person was acting on behalf of the mission and gathering information to further the legal representation. This can be done with a statement of purpose and of confidentiality.

The organization cannot expect confidentiality if it sets up a team comprised of internal personnel and people hired or on loan from other organizations. If the process sounds complicated, it is. The team has to be set up carefully (and even then, confidentiality is not guaranteed.)

To protect the investigation, consult with counsel to see what the standard for attorney-client privilege is in your jurisdiction. Make sure each person on the team understands his or her confidential role in serving the mission by further the legal representation. Document that outside consultants or investigators are considered to be your representatives. Have team members sign statements of confidentiality.

In addition, make sure that liability issues are covered. The contract with an outside consultant, or between the organizations, should specify who should indemnify the outside consultant and what insurance covers the person.

Investigative Findings or Attorney Opinions

Attorneys may want to split their factual work and their opinions. For instance, attorneys may create two memos from each interview. The first, a factual memo, would contain only the witness' comments, and be discoverable. The second, an opinion memo, would contain only opinions and observations about the witness, such as appearance, demeanor, verbal skills, truthfulness, and other details. The second memo would have a much stronger privilege argument, and likely not be discoverable.

Similarly, an attorney could create a factual findings report, summarizing evidence gathered and which facts were found to be credible. Then separately, the attorney could write an opinion memo with the attorney's personal opinions and legal advice. Here, the second memo would be attorney-client privileged communications.

Joint Investigations and Multiple Organizations

Shared investigations between two organizations can be kept confidential. There is a rule called the "joint defense" or "common interest" rule that lets two parties share information with each other and keep it all under the same privilege. Why would they want to do that? One useful reason may be to run a joint investigation that is more financially efficient and to be able to share documents and information with each other to have a complete set of documents. Another important reason could be to share information about a perpetrator that ordinarily would bring a risk of defamation, in order to prevent others from being harmed.

The "common interest" or "joint defense" doctrine applies when two parties share confidential communications as part of an ongoing common enterprise, to further the enterprise.[39] There need not be actual litigation in progress, but the parties must have a common legal interest and be engaged in a common legal strategy. Some courts require an actual legal strategy, not just a shared desire for the same outcome.[40]

The basic form of the common interest doctrine was developed for the situation where the same attorney represented multiple persons, but the doctrine is not limited to that situation. It also applies when parties are represented by separate counsel but are engaged in a common legal enterprise. The required elements are usually an agreement of some sort; that the communication is given in confidence; and that a joint strategy is apparent.

The common interest doctrine varies a lot between jurisdictions. One more limited view is that there can be either actual litigation or potential litigation to trigger the common interest rule, but there must be at least a "palpable threat of litigation."[41] This common legal interest includes shared communication between various actual or potential co-defendants, or their attorneys, as long as the communication concerns common issues and would facilitate the mutual representations of the parties in possible legal proceedings.[42]

The common interest doctrine is only a way to keep communications privileged, not to make them privileged. In order for material to stay privileged under the common interest doctrine, it must be privileged in the first place.

Common interest provides a good approach for two organizations to work together. When a joint investigation is set up with a joint defense agreement (with either one counsel representing both organizations or counsel for each organization working in cooperation), the parties can communicate about an investigation without waiving the privilege. Where this is not in place, communications between the organizations are probably discoverable.

First, counsel must analyze which version of the doctrine applies in your jurisdiction, because the doctrine varies a lot. Next, the best approach to setting up the joint defense or common interest agreement is to have a written agreement between the parties defining the common interest, how broadly it extends, and the mutual intent of the parties to keep material privileged. This helps both to define the parties' intent to have a joint defense and to define the scope of that defense in case of later disputes.

Legal Issues for a Cross-Borders Investigation

Alleged wrongdoing that has taken place overseas may generate legal problems in more than one jurisdiction, as there could be civil liability or criminal penalties there. Litigation in different countries can vary a lot. There may be different types of legal professionals, such as the difference between attorneys in the U.S.; barristers, solicitors, and solicitor-advocates in the U.K.; and notaries in France. Procedural differences in courts may be significant, including the types of documents that must be produced. For instance, in a recent case involving Chinese law, the court held that because documents in China are not protected by attorney-client privilege or the work-product doctrine, they were discoverable.[43]

Ethical and privilege rules are different. Data protection issues may vary significantly, depending on the jurisdiction.

A mission that receives allegations of child abuse in a remote area may have a lot to navigate, between local legal issues and the different nationalities of organizations and people involved. It is a good idea to have reliable local counsel available for advice when there are problems— hopefully ahead of time, because engaging local counsel may require some paperwork for background checks and so forth. It is preferable if your regular general counsel and local overseas counsel are able to communicate, as there may be a need to coordinate with regards to decision-making and litigation.

When there have been allegations of child abuse, local counsel can explain what is required under local laws. This may vary depending on whether the case is current, whether the alleged victim is already an adult, or whether persons involved are still in the jurisdiction. Counsel can advise on issues of safety and cultural appropriateness. Counsel can also advise on local law with respect to terminating an individual's employment, which may be difficult to do in some countries (such as China) even for wrongdoing.

When an Attorney Conducts the Investigation

An attorney's investigation can be a legal service, encompassed by the privilege,[44] but the attorney must be acting in the role of a lawyer for this to be true. For instance, in one case, a law firm conducted the investigation, and a battle developed over whether the defendant had to disclose notes and memoranda from witness interviews, and even legal memoranda.[45] The question in the case was whether, when an attorney is performing investigative work, she is acting as an attorney for purposes of the privilege. The court decided that the law firm had also been hired to provide legal advice, and the privilege applied to the communications made and documents generated during the investigation. Even with respect to witnesses interviewed who were not employees of the defendant, the material created was protected as attorney work product.

If the investigation takes place in conjunction with providing legal services, the material created by the investigation is privileged. If the client wants the attorney to use legal expertise and the "trained eyes of an attorney" in conducting an investigation, the investigation becomes legal work.[46] Generally, the courts will agree that an attorney brings special training and skills to the investigation and can then give legal recommendations.[47] If an outside attorney does the work solely as an investigator, but is not providing legal services, there will be no attorney-client privilege.[48]

If an attorney performs investigative work, the attorney should handle interviews and documents in a way that shows he and his staff intend to keep the attorney-client privilege intact and intend to create work product. If this is so, the material is likely protected.

When using an attorney to perform the investigation, particularly when general defense counsel is not involved, the engagement letter for the investigation should be a legal engagement letter, not a letter more reflective of a private investigative firm.[49] It should provide that the representation will include legal services. For instance, it should state that the client is retaining counsel to develop factual information for the purpose of providing legal advice. This means the attorney should be able to give legal nuance to the results of the investigation as well as defending the privileges.

Having an attorney perform the actual investigation creates the strongest work product protection for the information, because of the attorney's direct involvement.

Audio Recordings of Interviews and Privilege

Audio recordings may or may not be discoverable, depending on the jurisdiction, and how they are taken. Any time an interview is recorded, the organization should assume that it may have to be produced. The degree to which recorded interviews are protected will depend on whether the interview is more of a "witness statement," or on the other hand is more closely directed by the attorney or the attorney's representative.

In some jurisdictions, "witness statements" are not work product.[50] A "witness statement" can include a recording or a transcript of an oral statement.[51] For instance, a "recording of a statement made by a witness without any questions by the interviewer is clearly discoverable."[52] "At the other extreme, a recording is not discoverable if it only contains comments by the attorney concerning his trial strategy or opinions of the strength and weaknesses of the case."[53] If the recording falls between the two extremes, parts could be discoverable. It is less likely to be discoverable if it is material that helps the attorney to prepare for trial.[54]

Courts may be moving toward protecting recorded statements obtained through an attorney-directed interview. One court held that such a recording might even have absolute protection because it reflects an attorney's mental processes, but should at least have a qualified privilege, which protects the attorney's industry and efforts.[55] Of course, even if the tapes are protected by the work-product doctrine, if the plaintiff has a substantial need for the information, and it would be an undue hardship to get it through other means, he or she may be entitled to it anyway.

If recordings are of privileged information, the recordings themselves will also be privileged, such as recordings of discussions with counsel, which would be attorney-client privileged.[56]

When a recorded interview is done at the request of the attorney, and the person doing the interview acts as the agent of the attorney, the recording may be privileged.[57] The test is whether the document (or recording) "came into existence as a part of a communication to the attorney," which would be the case if it were made at the direction of an attorney.

In one case, the recording of an interview of a defendant made under hypnosis was privileged, because the hypnotist had been hired by the attorneys.[58] In another case, recorded interviews with several minors who were victims of child abuse were protected under the work product "privilege," despite the fact that the interviews were done for the previous criminal case, and the prosecuting attorney was present. The court held that the presence of essential third parties did not negate the privilege.[59] In another case, the plaintiff tried to get discovery of the recorded interview by the insurance carrier of the truck driver responsible for the accident. The court held that the interview was conducted in anticipation of litigation. It was appropriate to provide a written summary of the interview but to withhold the actual recording.[60]

As a practical matter, when an attorney is not involved, and there will be no effort to keep investigations privileged, standard interview questions can be used, with or without a recording.

When an attorney is involved, consult with the attorney on what interviews are to be done, and have the attorney review and make suggestions on the questions to be asked, with a view toward giving legal advice on the investigation. The material is more likely to be protected if it is prepared at the direction of counsel in anticipation of litigation, if it is then turned over to counsel, and if it is used in legal analysis.[61]

In addition, if you would like the material to be privileged, interviewees should not be asked to review notes or summaries of their interview, or to sign a statement or transcript. Doing so may confirm that it is a witness statement rather than attorney work product. Instead, if desired, they can sign a witness affidavit.

Attorneys as Fact Witnesses

While work product protection is stronger when an attorney conducts the investigation, attorney-client privilege is most likely to apply when outside defense counsel supervises the investigation for the purpose of giving legal advice but does not conduct the investigation directly.

If an attorney does the investigation as an attorney and gives legal advice about defense strategy to the organization, the attorney is arguably not an impartial outsider, for purposes of defusing criticisms of bias. Thus, the attorney should avoid roles that may be conflicting. Also, like any interviewer, an attorney doing the investigation is a potential fact witness. In short, an attorney conducting the interview should not be the organization's general attorney.

These difficulties can be avoided by defining the "legal advice" in the engagement letter as bringing the attorney's knowledge of the law and experience to carrying out the investigation in an impartial and neutral way.

In terms of privilege and legal advice, the best formulation uses attorneys in two roles. First, organizations may hire experienced attorneys to conduct the investigation. Work product is strongly protected, and there is also attorney-client privilege. These outside attorneys use their knowledge of the law and experience to generate factual reports, which are delivered to general counsel.

The entire investigation takes place under the supervision and request of your general counsel, who finalizes the report by drafting the substantive legal advice for which the investigation was carried out. The general counsel is not involved with the fact-finding but gives legal advice and direction for the organization.

If you must assert as an affirmative defense that the investigation was reasonable, you will be waiving attorney-client privilege, but only the privilege of the investigating attorney. Your defense counsel's advice will still be protected.

Do Religious Organizations Have Any First Amendment Rights Over Their Documents?

Religious organizations have extensive constitutional rights to carry out their own internal affairs and discipline, and decisions based on spiritual principles are shielded from intrusion from the courts. There is a strong argument that the courts should not even be looking at documents created to carry out religious decisions.

For instance, a child abuse investigation and subsequent actions may be supported by strong theological principles. Biblical principles may support behavioral standards in HR investigation and disciplinary decisions. This should be built into the organization's policy documents.

Any time an organization is doing investigations or taking disciplinary action based on spiritual principles, it is wise to say so in the documents triggering the investigation as well as in any reports. This will make it easier to claim the religious privileges. While the religious privileges are not as clear-cut as attorney-client privilege or work product, they should apply whether or not an attorney is involved, and whether or not litigation is anticipated. Also, they may be helpful in litigation strategy.

ACKNOWLEDGMENTS

I would like to acknowledge Telios Law employees and other expert consultants who have contributed to the research and writing of this work, including the following:

A.R. Ascano, J.D., M.S., L.P.C., who contributed research and information about memory and trauma

R. P. Ascano, Ph.D., L.P., D.P. Min.
Fellow, American College of Forensic Psychology
Fellow, American Academy of Experts in Traumatic Stress (Emeritus)
Assist. Professor of Forensic Psychiatry, UND, School of Medicine, Depart. of Psychiatry and Behavioral Science (Emeritus)
With thanks for information about research and memory and trauma

Joseph B. Brown, Esq., attorney with Telios Law
Dr. Roger L. Dixon, co-author of Appendix B
Dana DiDomenico, Esq., attorney with Telios Law
Daniel M. Geraghty, Esq., attorney with Telios Law
David B. Sidebotham, Creative Director of Telios Teaches
Rebecca M. Sidebotham, illustrator for cover and chapter headings and Marketing Director for Telios Law

ENDNOTES

Introduction

1   Isaiah 42:6–7.

Chapter 1: Reports and Complaints

1   Matthew 18:15–18.

2   Kirk O. Hanson, *How Leaders Should Handle Incidents of Sexual Abuse*, Markkula Center for Applied Ethics (Oct. 1, 2002), https://www.scu.edu/ethics/focus-areas/more/resources/how-leaders-should-handle-sexual-abuse-incidents/.

3   See, e.g., *Frederick v. Sprint/United*, 246 F.3d 1305 (11th Cir. 2001) (noting how an employer's unclear complaint procedure and notice of policies may impact the availability of an affirmative defense); *see also Franks v. Chitwood*, 572 F. Supp. 3d 1304 (2021) (holding the same and finding that mere presence of a clear policy is insufficient as well).

4   *See Upjohn Co. v. United States*, 449 U.S. 383, 394–95 (1981); *Collardey v. All. for Sustainable Energy, LLC*, 406 F. Supp. 3d 977, 980–81 (D. Colo. 2019) (declining to compel an employer to provide documents generated by outside counsel in the course of an investigation because the documents were work product and attorney-client privileged).

5   *Id.*

6   Model Rules of Prof'l. Conduct R. 2.1 (2020).

7   *See Jones v. SEPTA*, 796 F.3d 323, 326 (3d Cir. 2015).

8   *See Id.*; *but see East v. Clayton Cnty., GA*, 436 F. App'x 904, 912 (11th Cir. 2011) (finding that an employer had a legitimate, non-discriminatory reason for placing an employee on unpaid leave

pending the outcome of an internal investigation); *Coclough v. Akal Sec., Inc.*, No. CV 16-2376 (BAH), 2022 WL 768469, at *21 (D.D.C. Mar. 13, 2022) (finding the same).

9   Leora F. Eisenstadt & Jennifer M. Pacella, *Whistleblowers need not apply*, 55(4) Am. B. Law J. 595 (2018).

Chapter 3: Structuring the Investigation

1   *Vasquez v. Empress Ambulance Serv., Inc.*, 835 F.3d 267, 276 (2d Cir. 2016).

2   *See Bradley v. Autozoners, LLC*, No. 4:20-CV-00337-BLW, 2022 WL 1422928, at *13 (D. Idaho May 4, 2022) (noting that the "[e]effectiveness of the employer's remedy will be measured by the twin purposes of ending the current harassment and deterring future harassment—by the same offender or others.") (citing *Fuller v. City of Oakland, Cal.*, 47 F.3d 1522, 1528 (9th Cir. 1995)).

3   *See Smith v. First Union Nat'l Bank*, 202 F.3d 234, 240 (4th Cir. 2000).

4   *Noonan v. Miller Mem'l Cmty. Home, Inc.*, 928 A.2d 626, 628 (Conn. Super Ct. 2007).

5   *Id.*

6   *See S.E.C. v. Microtune, Inc.*, 258 F.R.D. 310, 317 (N.D. Tex. 2009)(finding waiver of privilege where confidential documents produced in the course of an internal investigation were turned over to an outside party).

7   *Doe v. Roman Cath. Diocese of Brooklyn*, No. CIV. CCB-15-244, 2015 WL 1046086, at *2 (D. Md. Mar. 9, 2015).

Chapter 5: Building the Investigative Team

1   *Upjohn Co. v. United States*, 449 U.S. 383 (1981); this is a warning that clarifies to witnesses that the interviewer is an attorney and the organization is the client, not any individual.

Chapter 6: Investigation in Progress

1   *Bohnert v. Roman Catholic Archbishop of San Francisco*, 136 F. Supp. 3d 1094 (N.D. Cal. 2015).

2   15 U.S.C. § 1681a(y).

3   In a context of union representation, *Weingarten* Rights mean that an employee can have union representation during an interview. While ministries practically never have unions, the concept is one of fundamental fairness.

4   See 2 Corinthians 12:20; Exodus 23:1; James 4:11.

5   Which applies in European Union-related matters.

Chapter 7: Memory and Credibility Issues

1   William Hirst & Gerald Echterhoff, "Remembering in Conversations: The Social Sharing and Reshaping of Memories," *Ann. Rev. Psych.* (2012) 63: 55-79.

2   Guiliana A. Mazzoni et al., "Changing Beliefs About Implausible Autobiographical Events: A Little Plausibility Goes a Long Way," *J. of Experimental Psych.: Applied* (2001) 7(1): 51-59. DOI: 10.1037//1076-898X.7.1.51.

3   Daniel B. Wright et al., "Social Recognition Memory: The Effect of Other People's Responses on Previously Seen and Unseen Items," *J. of Experimental Psych.: Applied* (2005) 11(3): 201.

4   Juliane Sachschal et al., "Differential effects of poor recall and memory disjointedness on trauma symptoms," *Clinical Psych. Science* (2019): 7(5), 1032-1041.

5   Fiona Gabbert et al., "Memory Conformity: Can Eyewitnesses Influence Each Other's Memories for an Event?" 17(5) *Applied Cognitive Psychology* (2003): 533–543.

6   Tiamoyo Peterson et al., "Me Too! Social Modeling Influences on Early Autobiographical Memories," *Applied Cognitive Psychology, UC Irvine School of Law Research Paper No. 2008* (2008).

7   Lorraine Hope et al., "With a little help from my friends…":
    The role of co-witness relationships in susceptibility to
    misinformation," *Acta Psychologica* (2008).

8   Daniel B. Wright & Marianna E. Carlucci, "The response order
    effect: People believe the first person who remembers an event,"
    Psychon Bull Rev. (2011) 18: 805-812.

9   Matthew Reysen, "The effects of social pressure on false
    memories," *Memory & Cognition* (2007) 35(1): 59-65.

10 Albert Carlin & Stephanie O'Malley, "Neuropsychological
    Consequences of Drug Abuse," in I. Grant & K.M. Adams
    (Eds.) *Neuropsychological Assessment of Neuropsychiatric Disorders*
    (1996); T. Nelson et al., "Effect of acute alcohol intoxication
    on recall and on judgments of learning during the acquisition
    of new information" in G. Mazzoni and T.O. Nelson (Eds.),
    *Metacognitive and Cognitive Neurophysiology: Monitoring and
    Control Processes* (1999).

11 L.M. Williams, "Recall of Childhood Trauma: A Prospective
    Study of Women's Memories of Child Sexual Abuse," *Journal of
    Consulting and Clinical Psychology* (1994) 62:1167-1176.

Chapter 9: Wrapping Up the Investigation

1   One helpful approach is for an organization to have a policy in
    the Employee Handbook that violations of child safety policy will
    be revealed to future employers.

Chapter 10: Leadership Responsibilities, Restoration, and Reconciliation

1   Isaiah 42:6-7.

Appendix A: Alleged Offenders Strike Back

1   *Wells v. Xavier Univ. et al.*, 7 F.Supp.3d 746 (S.D. Ohio 2014).

Appendix B: Child Sexual Abuse and Biblical Ethics

1   Kirk O. Hanson, *How Leaders Should Handle Incidents of Sexual Abuse*, Markkula Center for Applied Ethics (Oct. 1, 2002), https://www.scu.edu/ethics/focus-areas/more/resources/how-leaders-should-handle-sexual-abuse-incidents/.

2   *See* Psalm 68:5; Deuteronomy 10:18.

3   Isaiah 61:8; Exodus 22:21-24.

4   Romans 13:1-4.

5   Mark 10:14.

6   Matthew 18:6.

7   Dan Prater, "Child Abuse: What should the Church do about it?" *Enrichment Journal* (2017), http://enrichmentjournal.ag.org/200803/200803_136_ChildAbuse.cfm.

8   Ezekiel 16:20-21.

9   Jude 4.

10 Romans 13:1-5.

11 1 Cor. 5-6.

12 Matt. 10:16.

13 John Jay College of Criminal Justice, *The Nature and Scope of Sexual Abuse of Minors by Catholic Priests and Deacons in the United States 1950-2002* (Washington: United States Conference of Catholic Bishops, 2004), 263.

14 The John Jay study in 2004 opines that "sexual offenders are a risk of reoffending for a long period of time." *See id.* However, Dr. R.P. Ascano has provided the following research-based points. Sexual recidivism decreases with age. *See* Howard E. Barbaree et al., "The Development of Sexual Aggression through the Life Span: The Effect of Age on Sexual Arousal and Recidivism among

Sex Offenders," 989. *Ann. N. Y. Acad. Sci.* (2003): 59-71; Robert A. Prentky et al., "Sexually Coercive Behavior: Understanding and Management," 989 Ann. N. Y. Acad. Sci. (2003); R. Karl Hanson, "Recidivism and Age: Follow-Up Data From 4,673 Sexual Offenders," *17 J. Interpers. Violence* (2002): 1046-1062.

Offenders with prior criminal records are more likely to offend again, and those with contact sexual offenses offended again at a higher rate. Researchers reviewed criminal records of 201 adult males convicted of possession, distribution, or production of child pornography, in order to identify potential predictors of subsequent offenses. The result indicates that offenders with prior criminal records are significantly more likely to offend again, both sexual and non-sexual. Also, those with contact sexual offenses were reconvicted at a higher rate. In 2.5 years, 17 percent of the sample re-offended; however only 6 percent committed new child pornography offenses and 4 percent committed contact sexual offenses. *See* Michael C. Seto et al., "The Criminal Histories and Later Offending of Child Pornography Offenders," *17 Sex Abuse* (2005): 201-210.

Treatment can be effective for those who commit to respond to it. Significantly smaller proportions of treatment responders had recidivated (9 percent), compared to the treatment nonresponders (15 percent). Ths amounts to a 40 percent reduction in recidivism in those who had responded to treatment. Anthony R. Beech et al., "Comparing Recidivism Rates of Treatment Responders/ Nonresponders in a Sample of 413 Child Molesters Who Had Completed Community-Based Sex Offender Treatment in the United Kingdom," *56 Int J Offender Ther Comp Criminol, (2012):* 29-49.

Post-conviction and post-treatment polygraph maintenance can be used to monitor risk of potential sexual-contact recidivism to further decrease the risk to public safety.

15   John 10:11.

16   Eric Barreto, *Commentary* on "Matthew 18:15-20," *Working Preacher* (2014), http://www.workingpreacher.org/preaching. aspx?commentary_id=2164.

17   *Child Abuse and Matthew 18: The Dangers Of Distorting Scripture*, GRACE (May 10, 2013), http://www.netgrace.org/ resources/2015/4/9/child-abuse-and-matthew-18-the-dangers-of-distorting-scripture.

18   Matthew 18: 6, 10.

19   Deuteronomy 22:25.

20   Joshua 7:18.

21   2 Samuel 13.

Appendix C: Attorney-Client Privilege and Work Product

1   *Upjohn Co. v. United States*, 449 U.S. 383, 389 (1981).

2   *Id.* at 390.

3   *In re Grand Jury*, 475 F.3d 1299, 1903 (D.C. Cir. 2007).

4   *Simon v. G.D. Searle & Co.*, 816 F.2d 397, 404 (8th Cir. 1987); *see also Arkansas Oklahoma Gas Corp. v. BP Energy Co.*, No. 2:21-CV-02073, 2022 WL 1690266, *2 (W.D. Ark. 2022) (holding the same).

5   *King Drug Co. of Florence v. Cephalon, Inc.*, No. 2:06-cv-1797, 2013 WL 4836752 (E.D. Pa. Sep. 11, 2013).

6   Restatement (Third) of the Law Governing Lawyers § 68 (2000).

7   *United States v. Ghavami*, 882 F.Supp. 2d 532, 536 (S.D. N.Y. 2012).

8   *United States v. Finazzo*, 2013 WL 619572 (E.D.N.Y., Feb. 19 2013).

9   Tex. R. Evid. 503(a)(3).

10   *Renfield Corp. v. E. Remy Martin & Co. S.A.*, 98 F.R.D. 442, 444 (D. Del. 1982).

11   *Louis Vuitton Malletier v. Dooney & Bourke Inc.*, No. 04 Civ. 5316, 2006 WL 3476735, at *16-17 (S.D.N.Y. Nov. 30, 2006).

12   Michael C. Miller & Richard Rondoux, "Foreign In-House
     Counsel Communications," *New York Law Journal*, March 8,
     2012.

13   *Farzan v. Wells Fargo Bank*, No. 12 Civ. 1217 RJS, 2012 WL
     6763570 (S.D.N.Y. Dec. 28, 2012).

14   *In re Vioxx Prod. Liab. Litig.*, 501 F.Supp.2d 789, 797 (E.D.La.
     2007).

15   *Id.* at 798.

16   Case C-550-07 P. *Akzo Nobel Chem. v. European Comm'n*, Celex
     No. 607J 0550 (Sept. 14, 2010).

17   *Belgacom*, Case No. 2011/MR/3, Brussels Court of Appeals
     (March 5, 2013).

18   *Upjohn*, 449 U.S. at 391.

19   *In re Monsanto Co. et al.*, 998 S.W.2d 917, 922 (Tex. App. 1999)
     (quotes omitted).

20   *In re USA Waste Mgmt. Res.*, 387 S.W.3d 92 (Tex. App. 2012).

21   *Ghavami*, 882 F. Supp. 2d at 538.

22   An example of an appropriate *Upjohn* warning, issued by the
     American Bar Association's White Collar Crime Committee
     Working Group, follows: I am a lawyer for Corporation A.
     I represent only Corporation A, and I do not represent you
     personally. I am conducting this interview to gather facts in order
     to provide legal advice for Corporation A. This interview is part
     of an investigation to determine the facts and circumstances
     of X in order to advise Corporation A how best to proceed.
     Your communications with me are protected by the attorney-
     client privilege. But the attorney-client privilege belongs solely
     to Corporation A, not you. That means Corporation A alone
     may elect to waive the attorney-client privilege and reveal our
     discussion to third parties. Corporation A alone may decide to
     waive the privilege and disclose this discussion to such third

parties as federal or state agencies, at its sole discretion, and without notifying you. In order for this discussion to be subject to the privilege, it must be kept in confidence. In other words, with the exception of your own attorney, you may not disclose the substance of this interview to any third party, including other employees or anyone outside of the company. You may discuss the facts of what happened but you may not discuss this discussion.

23   *In re Refco Inc. Sec. Litig.,* 08 CIV. 3089 JSR, 2012 WL 678139 (S.D.N.Y., Feb. 28, 2012); *Muriel Siebert & Co., Inc. v. Intuit, Inc.,* 8 N.Y.3d 506, 511 (2007).

24   *In Re Avantel, S.A.,* 343 F.3d 311, 321 n. 11 (5th Cir. 2003).

25   *Koss v. Palmer Water Dep't,* 977 F. Supp. 2d 28 (D. Mass. October 7, 2013).

26   *Hickman v. Taylor,* 329 U.S. 495, 511 (1947).

27   *Ghavami,* 882 F. Supp. 2d at 540.

28   Tex. R. Civ. Pro. 192.5.

29   *Smith v. Coulombe,* No. 2:11-cv-531-SU, 2013 WL 428363 (D. Or. Feb. 4, 2013).

30   *In re Grand Jury Subpoena,* 357 F.3d 900, 910 (9th Cir. 2003).

31   *Farzan v. Wells Fargo Bank,* No. 12 Civ. 1217(RJS)(JLC), 2012 WL 6763570 (S.D.N.Y. Dec. 28, 2012).

32   *In re Baptist Hospitals,* 172 S.W. 3d 136 (Tex. App. 2005).

33   *In re Monsanto Co.,* 998 S.W.2d 917, 923 (Tex. App. 1999).

34   *In re Kaiser Aluminum and Chem. Co.,* 2114 F.3d 586, 593 (5th Cir. 2000).

35   *In re Energy XXI Gulf Coast, Inc.,* No. 01-10-00371-CV, 2010 WL 5187730 (Tex. App. Dec. 23, 2010).

36   *Farzan,* 2012 WL 6763570.

37   *Smith v. Coulombe,* 2013 WL 428363.

38   *King Drug Co. of Florence,* 2013 WL 4836752, at *8–9.

39 *Ghavami*, 882 F. Supp. 2d at 537 (citing *Upjohn Co. v. United States*, 449 U.S. 383, 390 (1981)).

40 *In re Pacific Pictures Corp. v. United States Dist. Court*, 679 F.3d 1121, 1129 (9th Cir. 2012).

41 *In re Santa Fe Int'l Corp.*, 272 F.3d 705, 711 (5th Cir. 2001).

42 *Aiken v. Texas Farm Bureau Mut. Ins. Co.*, 151 F.R.D. 621 (E.D. Tex. 1993).

43 *Wultz v. Bank of China Ltd.*, 979 F. Supp. 2d 479 (S.D. N.Y. October 25, 2013).

44 *Better Government Bureau, Inc. v. McGraw*, 106 F.3d 582, 601 (4th Cir. 1997).

45 *Sandra T.E. v. South Berwyn School Dist.*, 600 F.3d 612, 617 (7th Cir. 2010).

46 *McGraw*, 106 F.3d at 602.

47 *In re LTV Sec. Litig.*, 89 F.R.D. 595 (N.D. Tex. 1981).

48 *Diversified Indus. v. Meredith*, 572 F.2d 596, 603 (8th Cir. 1977).

49 To this end, the attorney should be able to claim attorney-client privilege in that jurisdiction.

50 Tex.R.Civ.P. 192.5(c).

51 *Id.* at 192.3(h).

52 *Washington v. State*, 856 S.W.2d 184, 188 (Tex. Crim. App. 1993).

53 *Id.*

54 *Id.* at p. 189 (not allowing discovery of a recorded interview which was part of an investigation).

55 *Coito v. Superior Court*, 278 P.3d 860 (Cal. 2012).

56 *Ghavami*, 882 F. Supp. 2d at 541–44 (S.D.N.Y. 2012) (citing *Upjohn Co. v. United States*, 449 U.S. 383, 390 (1981)) (finding that recordings of discussions about communications with counsel were privileged, where that privilege was never waived).

57 *Burnett v. State*, 642 S.W.2d 765, 769 (Tex. Crim. App. 1982).

58 *Id.* at 770.

59 *E. W. v. Moody*, NO. 06-5253 FDB, 2007 WL 445962, at *4 (W.D. Wash. Feb. 7, 2007).

60 *Pcolar v. Casella Waste Sys.*, 59 A.3d 702, 708 (Vt. 2012).

61 *See Aiken v. Texas Farm Bureau Mut. Ins. Co.*, 151 F.R.D. 621 (E.D. Tex. 1993).

ABOUT THE AUTHORS

Theresa Sidebotham's earliest memories are from the mission field. She grew up as a Third Culture Kid, experiencing almost every kind of school environment. She and her husband met at Wheaton College, and their four sons were born in three different countries, due to their parents' military and missions experiences. After they returned to the U.S., her husband stayed in ministry and Theresa went to law school. After a few years clerking at the Colorado Court of Appeals, Theresa worked with a large law firm's religious institution group's practice before she founded Telios Law. Theresa is now a grandmother, which makes her even more passionate about child safety.

Telios Law advises organizations in the U.S. and internationally, with a focus on religious and nonprofit law. Theresa advises on numerous misconduct investigations involving child abuse, workplace misconduct, and spiritual abuse. She also created Telios Teaches to provide online training for ministries aimed at preventing child abuse and toxic work cultures.

Rooted in the belief that legal solutions should bring healing and life, Telios Law staff strive to support, confront, and restore the spiritual health of the ministries they serve. They recognize that toxic abuses of power can leave people traumatized and divided, morals compromised, and the truth lost. Abuse or misconduct in ministry workplaces can cause a myriad of harms, including spiritual, emotional, and physical trauma.

Telios Law staff believe that those who have been harmed should have their stories heard in a caring and compassionate space, as a first step to healing. By actively seeking the truth and bringing forward the stories of survivors, Telios Law investigations help organizations create and maintain a safe work culture where misconduct is vigorously addressed without partiality or retaliation. Telios Law believes that well-conducted investigations bring healing and help organizations grow spiritually. To accomplish this, Telios Law uses current investigative best practices, works with psychologists and other expert consultants to support mistreated individuals, and takes into account the effects of trauma and evidence-based practices. The ultimate goals of an investigation are to uncover truth, seek healing for survivors, and provide an opportunity for reconciliation.

Co-author on Appendix B: Child Sexual Abuse and Biblical Ethics

Dr. Roger L. Dixon served on the mission field for 34 years. In addition to his theological work, he was an early adopter of homeschooling for MKs and mentored young missionary families on how to protect their children from child sexual abuse.

Telios Law serves businesses, individuals, ministries, and churches, representing them in litigation, investigations, appeals, and alternatives to litigation, as well as giving legal advice on a variety of issues.

Lawsuits. Employment issues. Misconduct allegations. These legal conflicts can leave people divided, morals compromised, and the truth lost. Telios Law creates legal solutions that can help solve conflicts in ways that heal people and preserve their vision, and protect from liability, without compromising belief.

When we practice law in a way that prioritizes healing and reconciliation, it helps our clients build healthy, safe work environments.

Want to learn more? Enroll in the Telios Tip.
There's a lot to know about running things right. And there's very little time in which to learn it. Subscribe to Telios Tip for a monthly, hot take on important legal matters.

CONTACT
PO Box 3488
Monument, CO 80132
TEL: 855-748-4201
EMAIL: tell@telioslaw.com

Not even counting the financial devastation that lawsuits can cause, allegations can jeopardize your ministry's future by ending relationships, damaging your culture, and undermining your reputation.

Telios Teaches' concise, values-based training teaches from an Imago Deo (image of God) perspective helping your learners understand prevention and empowering them to fulfill their calling.

Employees are happier and healthier when they are protected with a values-based workplace culture that speaks to and preserves their core beliefs.

Navigating the Storm: Investigation Training
Allegations of misconduct can create liability and destroy relationships, but a misconduct allegation handled well protects the innocent. **Use the QR Code to enroll for free.**

CONTACT
PO Box 3488
Monument, CO 80132
TEL: 719-300-6968
EMAIL: info@teliosteaches.com

telios teaches

TRAINING FROM TELIOS LAW PLLC

CPSIA information can be obtained
at www.ICGtesting.com
Printed in the USA
JSHW022119130123
36248JS00003B/15

9 781959 099000